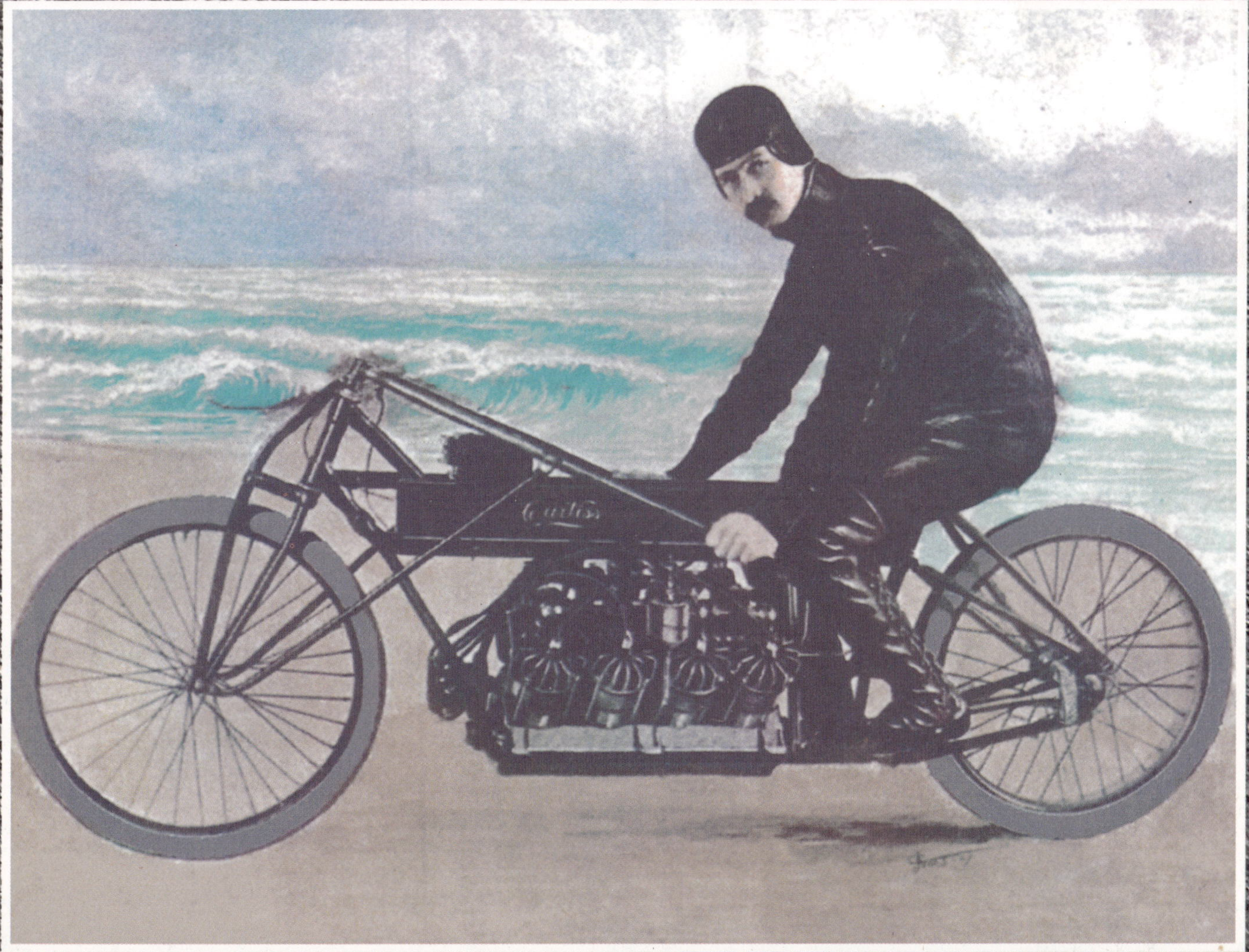

DAYTONA BIKE WEEK

Schiffer Publishing Ltd®

4880 Lower Valley Road Atglen, Pennsylvania 19310

Dedication

To my daughter, Laura, a long-time
Kawasaki motorcycle fan and owner.

COPYRIGHT © 2008 by Donald Spencer
Library of Congress Control Number: 2008926769

This book is comprised mainly of photographs taken by the author; illustrations, photographs and postcards from the author's collection; and Dover Publications, Inc. drawings on pages 7, 8 (center), 11 (bottom), and 23 (center). Clip art throughout the book is from BigStockPhotos.com.

Type set in Zurich BT with Clarendon.
ISBN: 978-0-7643-2977-7 | Printed in China

Schiffer Books are available at special discounts for bulk purchases for sales promotions or premiums. Special editions, including personalized covers, corporate imprints, and excerpts can be created in large quantities for special needs. For more information contact the publisher:

PUBLISHED BY Schiffer Publishing Ltd.
4880 Lower Valley Road Atglen, PA 19310
Phone: (610) 593-1777; Fax: (610) 593-2002
E-mail: Info@schifferbooks.com

For the largest selection of fine reference books on this and related subjects, please visit our web site at **www.schifferbooks.com**. We are always looking for people to write books on new and related subjects. If you have an idea for a book please contact us at the above address.

This book may be purchased from the publisher. Include $5.00 for shipping. Please try your bookstore first. You may write for a free catalog.

IN EUROPE, Schiffer books are distributed by:
Bushwood Books
6 Marksbury Ave. Kew Gardens
Surrey TW9 4JF England
Phone: 44 (0) 20 8392-8585;
Fax: 44 (0) 20 8392-9876
E-mail: info@bushwoodbooks.co.uk
Website: www.bushwoodbooks.co.uk
Free postage in the U.K., Europe; air mail at cost.

CONTENTS

ABOUT THE AUTHOR

Donald D. Spencer is the author of over 250 books. For the past several years, he has been writing history books about Florida's cities, rivers, attractions, beaches, animals, forts, and plantations. He has lived in the Daytona Beach area since 1962 and has been photographing biker events there for the past 20 years.

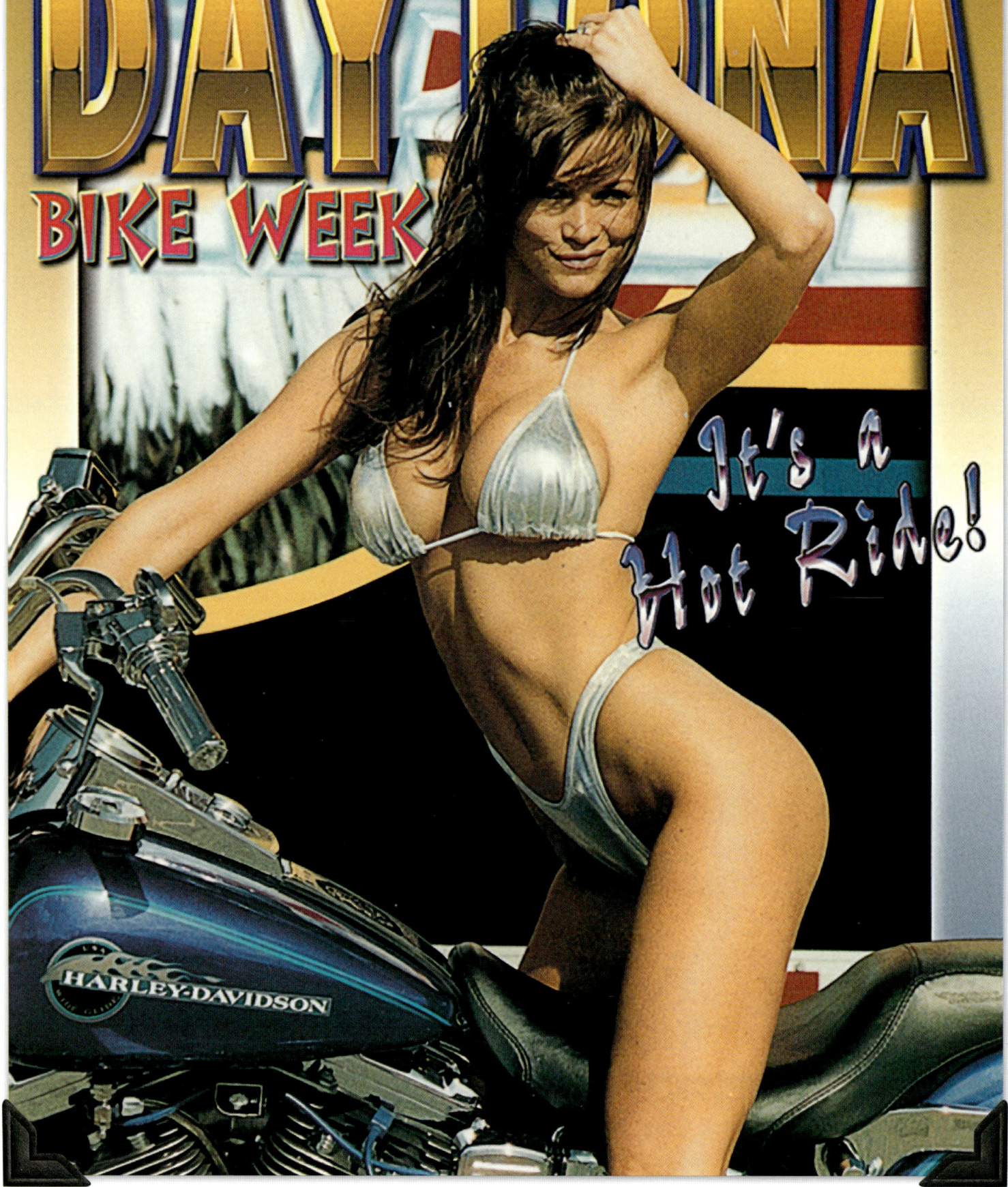

The love affair between Daytona Beach and motorcycle enthusiasts dates back to 1937, when the first running of the Daytona 200 Race was held on a mile-and-a-half of incredible beach and coastal road. It was a 3.2 mile course that had to be run at low tide, with two 180-degree turns of banked sand. It became immensely popular. In 1942, however, the American Motorcycle Association suspended the race in the interests of national defense during World War II. While the official race was suspended, locals and visitors turned out each year for an unofficial event that became known as Bike Week. When the official racing event resumed in 1947, the Daytona 200 was on a longer beach/road course, and in 1961, the race was moved to the Daytona International Speedway.

In 1986, the Daytona Beach Chamber of Commerce established an annual Bike Week festival, which, over the years, has become a major local event. Each year, around half of a million motorcycle enthusiasts visit the Daytona Beach area for Bike Week events.

Bike Week has been and is Daytona Beach's version of a motorized carnival, and has become the largest annual party of the city and surrounding communities. The event, held each spring, encompasses many sport racing events at the Daytona International Speedway and sideline biker events around the local area. Biketoberfest, a smaller version of Bike Week, is held each fall.

This scrapbook captures the history of Bike Week and Biketoberfest and is brought alive with roughly 400 photographs, postcard views, illustrations, racing programs and brochures, and posters from days gone by.

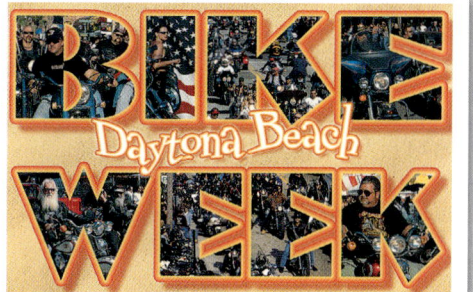

Postcards from the Bike Week festival, which has become the largest annual party of the city and surrounding communities.

A walk down Main Street gives everyone a view of every variety of Harley-Davidson bikes imaginable, from stock bikes to highly modified customs.

IN THE BEGINNING

Motorcycle history can be traced to November 10, 1885, when a bizarre-looking mechanical contraption traveled six miles through the German countryside. Paul Daimler, son of the machine's inventor, German engineer Gottlieb Daimler, drove a one-cylinder motorized bicycle from the village of Cannstatt to the town of Unterturkheim and back at an average speed of fifteen miles per hour. With its wooden frame, stabilizer "training wheels" and saddle-like seat, it looked very little like a modern motorcycle. Nonetheless, it was an improvement over earlier attempts, and heralded the beginning of a new industry.

Another pioneer in the development of the motorcycle was Count Albert De Dion of France, who built both bicycle-and tricycle-type vehicles with his partner Georges Bouton. During the early period of motorcycle manufacture, many companies sprang up to build complete vehicles or components such as engines. Hundreds of motorcycle brands were on the market during the first years of the twentieth century.

By 1900, daring young men and women with a budding interest in gas-powered machines found a variety of motorcycles available to them. From 1900 through 1903, small companies sprang up around Europe and North America, offering their wares to riders everywhere.

The Thomas Auto-Bi and the Orient became the first commercially produced motorcycles built in number in the United States. These motorcycles set the style for most of the early American motorcycles to follow. The first motorcycles, as well as automobiles, were greeted with the angry suggestion, "Get a horse!"

Gottlieb Daimler was the German designer of the first motorcycle, which was produced in 1885. It was constructed of a wooden frame and used a gasoline engine with hot-tube ignition,which could turn at the enormous rate of 800 RPM. Daimler's assistant William Maybach, rode the machine in 1886, but Daimler than turned to four wheels and abandoned the motorcycle.

1899 De Dion Bouton. Another pioneer in the development of the motorcycle was Count Albert De Dion of France, who built both bicycle- and tricycle-type vehicles with his partner George Bouton. De Dion machines were powered by single-cylinder engines ranging in size from 120-CCs to 500-CCs. The motorbike shown here had a 270-CC engine, which was rated at 1½ HP at 1800 RPM.

Iver Johnson bike.

In 1904, Glenn H. Curtiss, an inventor and mechanic from New York, made the first official recorded mile-a-minute speed record on a motorcycle. In 1907, Curtiss returned to the Ormond-Daytona Beach measured mile racecourse and, on his V-8 powered motorcycle, ran the racecourse in 26 seconds, at 136.3 MPH. Curtiss, who once slept in the Ormond Garage alongside his motorcycle, obtained worldwide fame and fortune. He died in 1930 at the age of 52.

1924 BSA "Round Tank." BSA began to produce motorized bicycles in 1906 and within a few decades it was Great Britain's largest motorcycle manufacturer. The 1924 "Round Tank" had a single-cylinder, 250-CC, four-stroke engine producing 2¼ HP. The 170-lb. machine could attain a speed of 45 MPH.

On January 24, 2007, Joe Meade of the Glenn H. Curtiss Museum, located in Hammondsport, New York, rode a 1909 Curtiss V-twin motorcycle during the 100th anniversary re-enactment of Glenn Curtiss' speed record ride. On January 24, 1907 Curtiss became the "fastest man alive." The Curtiss Restoration Shop in New York restored an original two-cylinder Curtiss motorcycle to running condition for the run.

BRITISH AND GERMAN BIKES

TRIUMPH Triumph is the longest-lived British motorcycle which was first produced in 1902 and is still surviving in 2008. The firm began with the usual motorized bicycle and moved on to some famous models. The original name of the company was the Triumph Bicycle Company. It was founded in 1897 by German immigrants Siegfried Bettman and Mauritz Schulte. In 1902 they equipped one of their bicycles with a Minerva engine, and a great name in motorcycle history was born.

NORTON The most famous make of English bike, the Norton reigned supreme in road racing for 30 years. The company began in 1902, originally with imported engines, and went on to win the first Tourist Trophy (TT) race in 1907. After that Norton never looked back and continued winning until the 1950s. Norton motorcycles were highly successful at the racetrack. Founder James Norton gained a reputation for rapid racing bikes and strong, reliable roadsters.

An advertising brochure for the 1936 Triumph motorcycle range.

A Triumph Daytona motorcycle.

BSA Birmingham Small Arms (BSA) Company began to produce motorized bicycles in 1906 and within a few decades it was Great Britain's largest motorcycle manufacturer. In the years after World War II it was the largest in the world, producing over 75,000 bikes in some years during the 1950s. BSA built several light, fast and agile bikes during the 1960s and 1970s. BSA motorcycles, together with Triumph and Norton models, comprised a trio of classic British sport bikes that dominated the world market until Japanese motorcycles began their climb during the 1960s. The company finally ended production in 1971 after a proud history of over 60 years making motorcycles. In 1979 the name was brought back on mopeds made by Norton-Villiers-Triumph.

BMW One of the great success stories of the motorcycle industry, this German company produced the original flat twin horizontally-opposed design by Max Friz in 1923. BMW began as an airplane-engine manufacturer and in 1920 ventured into the motorcycle engine business. They were so successful at this that they created their own motorcycle. Today, BMW is the only remaining once-massive German motorcycle industry.

INDIAN, HARLEY-DAVIDSON, EXCELSIOR, AND BUELL

INDIAN In 1901, partners Oscar Hedstrom and George Hendee began producing Indian motorcycles. The 1905 Indian single-cylinder model was one of the first in a long line of popular and reliable American motorbikes. Its 288-CC engine produced 2.5 HP, allowing the 115-lb. cycle to reach a speed of 30 MPH. The Indian company later adopted the two-cylinder V-twin, and continued building motorcycles until the 1950s. Many of the classic machines they produced are among the most highly prized by today's vintage motorcycle collectors.

In 1948, Indian built the Daytona Sports Scout; one of these bikes took Floyd Emde to victory in that year's Daytona 200 Race.

From their start until the last production motorcycle was built in 1952, Indians have been a proud part of American motorcycle history. The company later resumed production of machines and today is again a popular maker of American motorcycles.

HARLEY-DAVIDSON One of the most enduring icons of American popular culture is the Harley-Davidson motorcycle, affectionately referred to as the "Hog." The Harley-Davidson Motor Company was formed by the partnership of William S. Harley and Arthur Davidson in 1903. Initial sales were slow, but by 1907 annual sales had risen to 150 motorcycles. Harley was very interested in manufacturing quality machines. Craftsmanship and reliability were eMPHasized in early advertising brochures. By 1911, the production of Harley machines was nearly 5,000. Two years later the Bell Telephone Company started replacing its horse and wagon work rigs with Harley-Davidson motorcycles with side cars.

During World War I, the U. S. Army had more Harley-Davidson motorcycles than all other makes combined. During 1913 to 1918, Harley-Davidson enjoyed supremacy in racing. During the 1915 season the Harley-Davidson racing team started winning every major race. In 1915 the Harley-Davidson factory produced 20,000 motorcycles for the U. S. Army.

After World War I, however, motorcycle production went into a downward spiral. In 1920, Harley-Davidson produced 23,000 motorcycles while the Ford Motor Company manufactured eight million automobiles. Henry Ford had produced an automobile (Model T) that was priced at only one hundred dollars more than a Harley-Davidson motorcycle. It was obvious that everyone wanted to drive and own a Tin Lizzie. No one needed to buy a motorcycle for cheap transportation any longer.

But the desire to own a motorcycle for aesthetic and collector reasons kept Harley-Davidson alive, and today they are the most recognizable and cherished motorcycles in the world.

Harley-Davidson advertisement, 1931.

Harley-Davidson motorcycles.

Harley-Davidson 1928 Sales Catalog.

A Harley-Davidson Touring bike.

Harley-Davidson 1930 Sales Catalog.

HARLEY-DAVIDSON IN WORLD WAR II

With the start of World War II in Europe in 1939, the motorcycle was adopted for military use. An initial order of 5,000 Harley-Davidson Model WLAs for the British Army eventually led to a total production of over 90,000 vehicles for all the Allied forces. The Harley's primary virtue was its ruggedness and reliability; it performed its duty well, and was a valuable asset to the war effort.

1943 Harley-Davidson Model WLA, ordered in mass quantities for the British Army during WWII.

EXCELSIOR Four different American, British, and German companies have used the Excelsior name. The British one was the longest-lived, manufacturing from 1896 to 1964. The first German company at Brandenburg began in 1901 and lasted until 1939. The other German Excelsior lasted only one year (1923-24) in Munich, where it produced a 250-CC two-stroke machine. The fourth Excelsior, the American company, was based in Chicago. It began as part of the Schwinn Company in 1907. They developed many fine racing machines including the 1913 Excelsior Auto Cycle. Excelsior continued to build motorcycles until 1931, when the Great Depression forced them out of business. Though their production life was fairly short, Excelsior bikes were in their day the third most popular American-made motorcycle, after Indian and Harley-Davidson.

BUELL Harley-Davidson's reluctance to build a sports bike has led many smaller firms and individuals to produce machines powered by the firm's V-twin engine. Among those is Erik Buell, a former road-racer and Harley-Davidson engineer, who designed and built an innovative, fully-faired bike which was successful in twin-cylinder racing in the 1980s. Buell's manufacturing facilities were located near Harley-Davidson's corporate headquarters in Milwaukee, Wisconsin, so Harley-Davidson remained in close contact with Buell. By 1998, Harley-Davidson had acquired 98 percent of Buell Motor Company and is using Buell to explore youth and sport bike markets with new models.

Buell motorcycle.

PROFESSIONAL MOTORCYCLE RACING

By 1908 motorcycle racing was rampant, and spectacular competitions were organized. The ¼- and 1/3-mile tracks were all were wooden structures, steeply banked at their bends to encourage high speeds. Every medium-sized city in America had a racetrack. Motorcycle teams were formed and leagues organized. Terrific rivalries resulted between teams and leagues. The tremendous speeds sometimes caused out-of-control machines which resulted in rider and spectator death and injury; by 1913, authorities called a halt to "motordrome madness" and banned "motorcycle races."

The motorcycle industry began to prosper again during World War I, and during the early 1920s professional motorcycle racing became popular. In 1923 riders formed the American Motorcycle Association to underline the sporting nature of motorcycles. As speeds increased many changes were made in the racing rulebooks. The depression of the 1930s caused all American motorcycle manufacturers to tighten their belts.

During the 1930s motorcycles became increasingly popular with the general public. Advances in engineering and technology allowed more comfortable, powerful bikes to be developed that were still affordable to the average working person. Harley-Davidson created one of their classic motorcycles in 1936 – the Model VLH. It featured their largest V-twin side-valve engine. They would produce overhead-valve engines for subsequent models, beginning with the famous "Knuckleheads," so-called because of their fist-shaped overhead valve rocket-arm covers. Also, it was one of the first machines to feature "crash guards" to protect the engine from damage in the event of a spill.

ITALIAN BIKES

The Italian motorcycle industry has a long history of building innovative, race-winning machines. Names such as Benelli, Gilera, Laverda, Moto Guzzi and Ducati are all associated with fast and powerful road and racing bikes.

DUCATI The Italian Ducati machine was made from 1950 onward, and was very successful in racing. The company began with small overhead valve machines under 250-CC and developed the desmodromic valve gear for racing. There were also production models and motocross versions, but since 1971 there have been much larger V-twins in the 750-and-up categories. The company is partly owned by the Italian government.

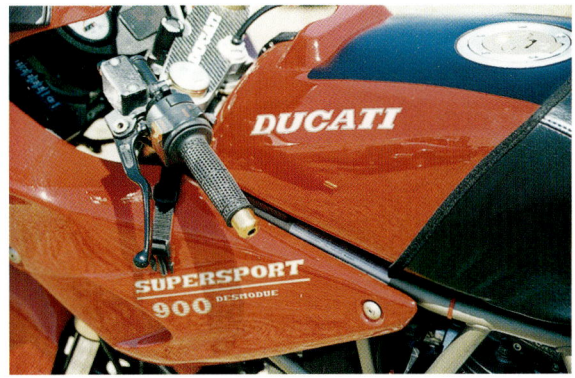

Ducati motorcycle.

Below, from top: Honda Super Hawk 996 motorcycle, Kawasaki Ninja motorcycle, and a Suzuki motorcycle.

JAPANESE BIKES

In the 1970s, 1980s, 1990s and into the 2000s, the Japanese superbikes manufactured by Honda, Kawasaki, Suzuki and Yamaha have dominated the Daytona 200 and Daytona Supercross Races. These companies are very competitive and are periodically introducing new, innovative, powerful racing bikes and sport bikes.

Today, Japan is the world's biggest producer of motorcycles in the world. The industry prides itself in providing different motorcycles for every corner of the market.

HONDA The world's largest motorcycle manufacturer was founded in 1946 by Soichiro Honda. In 1949 Honda and his 20 employees produced their first complete bike. By 1953 Honda had developed a more sophisticated bike, but revolutionized the motorcycle business in 1968 with the introduction of their four-cylinder CB750 Model. Honda's machine effectively ended the six-decade reign of British motorcycle domination.

KAWASAKI The motorcycle division forms a relatively small part of Kawasaki Heavy Industries, a vast firm that produces trains, boats, and planes. Kawasaki's involvement with bikes began in the 1950s when the industrial giant wanted to increase awareness of its name. In 1960 Kawasaki built its first complete bike and six years later moved into the big bike market. Kawasaki's Z1 was released in 1973 and dominated superbiking for much of the decade. Over the years Kawasaki has won many international racing championships.

SUZUKI Michio Suzuki set up a business manufacturing silk looms in 1909, and ran it until World War II. In 1952, problems in the silk loom industry led Suzuki to develop and sell a 36-CC two-stroke engine, which clipped to a bicycle frame. In 1954 the revived Suzuki firm launched its first complete bike. In 1967, Suzuki entered the big bike market and in 1971, produced its first true superbike. Suzuki continues to produce superbikes that compete well with bikes in the international marketplace.

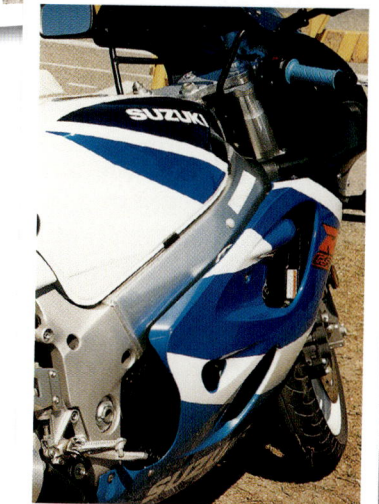

YAMAHA Torakusu Yamaha founded Nippon Gakki, which grew into one of the world's largest musical instrument manufacturers in 1897. In 1955 Nippon Gakki established the Yamaha company to build motorbikes, using machinery that had made aircraft propellers in World War II. Yamaha began establishing a reputation for quick, light, and reliable two-stroke bikes. Throughout the years Yamaha has produced many great superbikes and has won many racing championships.

Four motorbike aces with a formidable array of Indian bikes on the beach at Daytona Beach in 1909. Left to right: Walter Goerke, Oscar Hedstrom, Robert Stubbs and A. G. Chapple.

A. G. Chapple on the beach racecourse in Daytona Beach in 1909.

PIONEER RACING ON THE BEACH

The annual motorcycle race at Daytona Beach is one of the oldest continuous competition events in the two-wheeled sport. Daytona Beach first became linked with motorized sports because of its long, flat, hard-packed sand shoreline that made an ideal course for high-speed record runs in the early days of automobile and motorcycle manufacturing. Starting in 1903, several motorcycle speed records were made on the Ormond-Daytona Beach racecourse.

On January 28, 1904, Glenn H. Curtiss made the first officially recorded mile-a-minute on a motorcycle. Three years later Curtiss returned to the beach and roared his motorcycle with a big V-8 engine into the measured mile, tripping the clocks at an unofficial 136.3 MPH. A special edition of the Chicago Daily News had the headline, "FASTEST MILE ON EARTH," and a subhead stating, "Bullets Are The Only Rivals of Glenn Curtiss." Curtiss went on to become the first licensed pilot in America and, using the same V-8 motorcycle engine, made one of the first official airplane flights in the world. Then he went to Europe, and won the first air race in history. Curtiss continued his aeronautical research of takeoffs and landing on ships and became the acknowledged Father of Naval Aviation. Glenn Curtiss later contributed to the development of the Florida cities Hialeah, Miami, and Opa Locka.

On March 13, 1937, on the hard sand shoreline at Daytona Beach, Joe Petrali set a two-way average speed record of 136.183 MPH on a streamlined Harley-Davidson motorcycle. This measured-mile record still holds today as the fastest speed attained by a motorcycle on the sand. Petrali, one of Harley-Davidson's greatest racers, went on to win many national racing championships. Petrali retired in 1938 to become the flight engineer and chief service and maintenance man for Howard Hughes.

The Daytona International Speedway is the site of the Daytona 200 race, the Daytona Supercross races, bike manufacturers' displays, and other bike related events.

The start of a championship race at the Daytona International Speedway.

DAYTONA 200 RACE

The original motorcycle races in Daytona Beach were actually held on the beach, with riders trying to hold their bucking bikes through turns plowed into soft sand. Those were the days, and they went on for many years before a track was built and Daytona Beach racing became a paved roadrace event. In the early years the Daytona 200 Race was also called the "Handlebar Derby" by local racing fans. The sand dunes along the racecourse gave spectators a good view of the race. Watching the races was also about as dangerous as riding in them. There were no barricades or fences separating spectators from the racing bikes. Spectators occasionally would have to flee for their lives, scattering as an out-of-control bike left the course.

The original course south of Daytona Beach was 3.2 miles long, with a stretch down the beach, a 180-degree corner on sand, then a stretch along a narrow road (U.S. Highway A1A) which ran parallel to the beach behind the sand dunes and back to the beach via another 180-degree turn.

The first Daytona 200 Race took place on January 24, 1937 in front of some 15,000 spectators. From a field of ninety-eight riders the winner was Ed Kretz, Sr. from California, riding an Indian V-twin motorcycle and averaging 73.34 MPH.

The next two Daytona 200 Races (1938 and 1939) were won by Benny Campanale on Harley-Davidson bikes. The beach/road course was a rough one; the 1940 event saw only 15 of the original 77 starters still running at the end. Babe Tancrede won this race on a Harley-Davidson bike with a speed of 75.11 MPH.

In 1941 the Daytona 200 Race was won by Billy Mathews on a Norton bike with a speed of 78.08 MPH. From an economic standpoint, the Daytona 200 Race was the areas most important annual event during the years 1938 through 1941. Then, World War II intervened, and there were no races during 1942-1946. The sanctioning body of the Daytona 200, the American Motorcycle Association (AMA), stated that it was in the interest of national defense that the event be cancelled. But even though the racing event was "officially" called off, people still showed up for the "unofficial" party, known as Bike Week.

On February 24, 1947, the Daytona 200 Race resumed and was now promoted by the legendary Bill France of automobile and NASCAR fame. This race featured a record 176 motorcycle riders. The streets

of Daytona Beach were packed with motorcycles bearing license plates from all over America. Johnny Spiegelhoff won the race that year on an Indian bike at 77.14 MPH.

Daytona Beach was now becoming the center of American Motorcycling. In 1948, a new 4.1-mile beach/road course was built. Bleachers were built on the north and south ends of this course. Floyd Emde on an Indian bike won the Daytona 200 this year at an average speed of 84.01 MPH. This was also the year that saw the last victory by an Indian machine.

In 1949 over 2,000 bikers came to Daytona Beach for the eighth annual national championship races. Realizing the importance of the Daytona 200 Race and the motorcycling market in America, British motorcycle manufacturers—notably Norton—began to take an interest, and in that year Norton-mounted Dick Klamfoth set a race record at 86.42 MPH when he won the Daytona 200 in front of over 16,500 fans.

Norton bikes went on to scoop three more Daytona 200 victories in successive years. Billy Mathews was the driver in 1950, while Dick Klamfoth again claimed the victories in 1951 and 1952. In 1953, Paul Goldsmith won the Daytona 200 riding a Harley-Davidson at an average speed of 94.45 MPH.

The modern era of the AMA Grand National Series began in 1954, with the National Champion determined by the highest total number of points accumulated throughout the season. In that first year, Bobby Hill won the Daytona 200 Race on a BSA. The next six-years at Daytona Beach were dominated by Harley-Davidson bikes, the winners in order being Brad Andres, Johnny Gibson, Joe Leonard, Joe Leonard, Brad Andres, and Brad Andres a third time.

Harley-Davidson made a resounding sweep of the 1960 Daytona road races. In the Daytona 200, it was veteran Brad Andres, who scored his third Daytona victory while leading thirteen other Harley-Davidson racers to the top fourteen places. This was the last Daytona 200 Race on the beach/road course. The next year the famed race was moved from the hard-packed beach to a newly constructed racetrack. The new enclosed speedway, which is much safer for both drivers and spectators, would be the home of all future racing events in Daytona Beach.

In 1961 the Daytona 200 Race was transferred to the new Daytona International Speedway, with the main race supporting a number of motorcycling events over a full week for the first time. Roger Reiman of Kewanee, Illinois led every lap but the first on his Harley-Davidson to win the 200-mile National Championship on the Daytona International Speedway road course. Reiman averaged 69.25 MPH in the twisting, torturous 100-lap road race. His winning time was two hours, 53 minutes, 17.51 seconds.

Harley-Davidson riders took three of the first six places. A crowd in excess of 7,500 attended this race. Throughout the 1960s it was a straight battle between the 750-CC side-valve Harley-Davidsons and 500-CC OHV-paralleled twin Triumphs. Riding honors went to Reiman (four), Calvin Rayborn (two), with Don Burnett, Buddy Elmore, Gary Nixon and Ralph White all gaining single victories.

Perhaps the greatest accolade to symbolize Harley-Davidson's dominance of motorcycle competition in the late 1960s was the nickname

Daytona 200 action.

bestowed on its team of Class C dirt trackers and road racers. "The Wrecking Crew" was so powerful in 1968 that it won 18 of 23 National Championship races held that year, wrecking everyone else's hopes of having a winning season. The most stunning ride of the year was turned by team road racing ace Calvin Rayborn, as he rode his streamlined KR to victory at the Daytona 200-miler a full four miles ahead of the second place rider. Rayborn's win was one for the record books, as he ran the race at an average speed of 101.290 MPH, the first motorcycle to crack the 100-MPH barrier on the famed course. He also became the first racer to do it a second time when he won again in 1969, at an average speed over 100 MPH after having lapped the entire field.

In 1970 the American Motorcycle Association brought in European style rules, and Dick Mann won on a Honda CB750 at an average speed of 102.69 MPH. This race marked Honda's first Daytona 200 win. Mann repeated his success on a BSA Rocket Three the following year before Don Emde (1972) and Jarno Saarinen (1973) both won on 350 Yamaha two-strokes.

Since then the event has seen a galaxy of stars as victors, including Giacamo Agostini (1974), Gene Romero (1975), Johnny Cecotto (1976), Steve Baker (1977), Kenny Roberts (1978), Dale Singleton (1979), Patrick Pons (1980), Dale Singleton (1981), Graeme Crosby (1982), Kenny Roberts (1983 and 1984), Freddie Spencer (1985), Eddie Lawson (1986), Wayne Rainey (1987), Kevin Schwantz (1988) and John Ashmead (1989). Yamaha had the winning bikes from 1972 through 1984, and again in 1986; Honda bikes crossed the winning line in 1985, 1987, and 1989; in 1988, the winning bike was a Suzuki.

The 1990s saw another major rule change which brought a new look to the Daytona 200. Under the previous rules a machine had only to be suitable under American Motorcycle Association ruling. This was amended so that only road-based motorcycles could take part. That included machines built for the World Superbike Series, such as the Ducati V-twins and the entire line of Japanese four-cylinder models from Honda, Kawasaki, and Yamaha. Daytona 200 winners throughout the 1990s were: David Dadowski (Yamaha-1990), Miguel Duhamel (Honda-1991), Scott Russell (Kawasaki-1992), Eddie Lawson (Yamaha-1993), Scott Russell (Kawasaki-1994), Scott Russell (Kawasaki-1995), Miguel Duhamel (Honda-1996), Scott Russell (Yamaha-1997), Scott Russell (Yamaha-1998), and Miguel Duhamel (Honda-1999).

Mathew Mladin, a veteran racer from Australia, brought down the ending flags with spectacular victories in 2000 and 2001 editions of the motorcycle classic. He was riding a Japanese Suzuki bike. In 2002, Nicky Hayden rode his Honda motorcycle into Victory Lane in front of 40,000 racing fans. Miguel Duhamel won the race in 2003 on a Honda motorcycle. In 2004 Matthew Mladin rode a Suzuki bike to win the Daytona 200. Miguel Duhamel racked up his fifth Daytona 200 win on a Honda in 2005. The 2006 and 2007 races were won by Jake Zemke (Honda) and Steve Rapp (Kawasaki) respectively.

The Daytona 200 remains the race for the motorcycle manufacturers, riders, and most of all, the thousands of spectators who flock to Daytona Beach each spring. But enough about the race; you're here for the party.

BIKE WEEK

Perhaps it was the appeal of excellent weather, hard, sand beaches, or the excitement of that first motorcycle race on the beach that made Daytona Beach the home of Bike Week. Maybe it was the spirited activities surrounding the event that have kept motorcycle riders coming back. Whatever the reason, Bike Week has been a tradition since January 24, 1937—the inaugural running of the Daytona 200 Race. It has since become Daytona Beach's largest annual party. New Orleans has Mardi Gras; Tampa has the Gasparilla Festival; Key West has Fantasy Fest; Daytona Beach has Bike Week. Combined with many sporting events at Daytona International Speedway, Bike Week encompasses many sideline biker activities, from the Biggest Beer Belly contests to ladies' arm wrestling, biker parades to Best Bikini contests, and Best Tattoo contests to side shows.

Bike Week has been and is Daytona Beach's version of a motorized carnival. Although visitors are spread around the Daytona Beach area during this event for beach-going, shopping, and dining, most of the bikers are more interested in strutting their stuff along Main Street. Mean-looking dudes wearing black leather jackets mingle shoulder to tattooed shoulder on every last inch of the sidewalk. Most of the bikers are law-abiding citizens, and cause little concern to the local townspeople. Lines of patiently-queuing bikers seem to sit in stationary traffic all day. Most motorcyclists act just like their four-wheeled cousins in heavy traffic.

Bike Week is a big show, and what a show it is—the weirder the better. Obviously there are many who just ride a normal bike, wear a normal helmet, and blend with the crowd. But during Bike Week just about

Banners hung by manufacturers welcome bikers to Bike Week.

anything can be seen. Many bikers arrive in eye-popping costumes and ride their bikes down Main Street, posing for cameras all day long. Many costumed bikers park their bikes on Main, and though it may sound unbelievable, many bikers spend the whole week just queuing to get one of these coveted parking spaces that come with an audience.

Spectators will see almost everything: Harley bikes of all shades and hues, beautiful custom bikes next to ugly ones, vintage Indian bikes, old British bikes, military bikes, and countless one-of-a-kind special bikes of every size and description. Mixed up with the bikes are side attractions such as bikini-clad girls, sidewalk vendors, bottled water salesmen, donation collectors, many bearded and beer-bellied bikers – and lots of law enforcement personnel.

Bike Week has always had a flavor of its own. Sometime after World War II, the event began to take on a rugged edge. While the motorcycle races on the beach were organized, events surrounding the races were not. Relationships between bikers, local residents, and law officials continued to worsen over the years until Daytona Beach city organizations initiated action to improve and change the magnitude and scope of the event.

Because of their efforts, Bike Week is now a ten-day festival that expands throughout Volusia County and there are hundreds of events for motorcycle enthusiasts to enjoy. Bike Week is an annual event that enjoyed by hundreds of thousands of visitors, as well as locals and motorcycle enthusiasts worldwide.

In addition to the Daytona 200, Daytona Supercross and other races, bikers enjoy the festival atmosphere on Main Street, on Beach Street in downtown Daytona Beach, at Bruce Rossmeyer's Destination Daytona, and at many

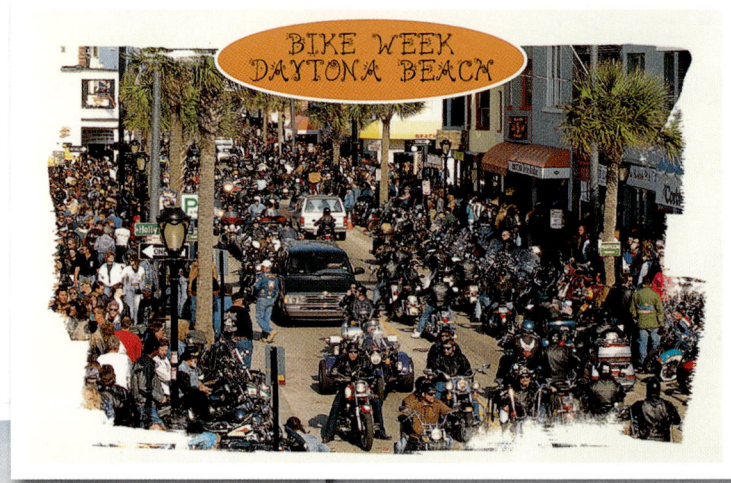

A postcard from the world's largest gathering of motorcyclists.

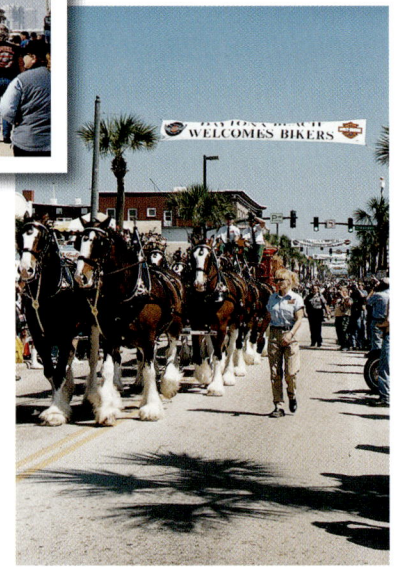

Bike Week crowd at the Daytona Bandshell, Bike Week's entertainment stage.

Budweiser Clydesdales marching on Main Street.

popular gathering spots along U. S. Highway 1 between Ormond Beach and New Smyrna Beach.

The Annual Bike Week in Daytona Beach remains the largest biker event and destination running, and it continues to grow. Only the events held in Sturgis, South Dakota and Laconia, New Hampshire come even close – but their combined attendance barely equals that of in Bike Week. While beer, food, crazy contests and biker merchandise always lures a few, the draw is and always has been the motorcycles, new and old, and the people that ride them, who come in every size, shape, color and gender to form a true brotherhood of motorcycle enthusiasts.

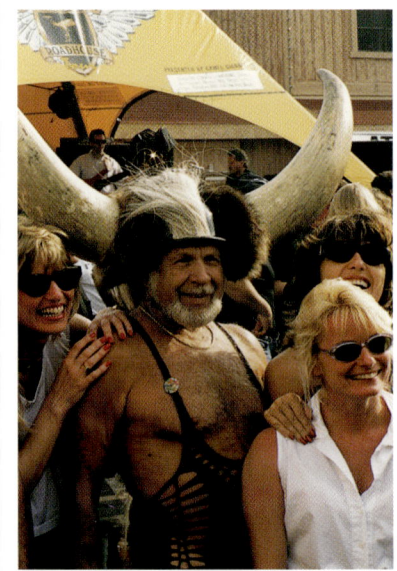

Entertainment on Main Street.

Gotta love a town that would post "MOTORCYCLES ONLY" on its busiest street.

POPULAR BIKE WEEK HANGOUTS

For many years the Boot Hill Saloon on Main Street has been where motorcycle enthusiasts gather to gander at each other's bikes, drink a little beer, hear a little music, and grab a little grub. This popular hangout is a destination for thousands of bikers.

New to the area is Bruce Rossmeyer's Destination Daytona, located on U. S. Highway 1 six miles north of Ormond Beach. It is the largest Harley-Davidson dealership in the world, and is surrounded by many activities during Bike Week. A lot of the activity that used to center on Beach Street has been transferred to Destination Daytona.

The Iron Horse Saloon, located on U. S. Highway 1 in Ormond Beach, was opened by Billy Stevens in the early 1980s. This is a popular Bike Week and Biketoberfest hangout that has a Wall of Death attraction, live music, many vendors, biker bars, and food establishments. Thousands of bikers patronize this exciting biker hangout each day.

The Cabbage Patch, another hangout located in Samsula just southwest of Daytona Beach, has an interesting history. This biker haven has also seen incarnations as a grocery store, and yes, as a cabbage field, since it has been in the Sopotnik family since 1926. The way the story goes, the family was having problems with the cabbage business, and Aunt Ollie, who managed the tavern at that time, plowed under the cabbages and opened the fields to bikers as a campground. Aunt Ollie became somewhat of a "den mother" to bikers years ago when they used to drag race on the dirt road near the tavern, then come in for a cold brew after the races. Her nephew, Ronnie Luznar, kept Aunt Ollie's "biker hangout" alive as a biker bar and kept the fields open for camping. Today, Aunt Ollie's famous hospitality has turned into a popular biker attraction that includes live music, a popular Coleslaw Wrestling Contest, bike displays, and lots of food and good times.

Located in a former fruit stand in New Smyrna Beach, Gilly's Pub 44 sits on a two-acre site bordered by a private lake. Owner Gilly Aguiar was the originator of the "Bike Bash" back in 1981. During Bike Week and Biketoberfest, bikers have been enjoying the Bash, great food, lots of camaraderie, and good times.

Wall painting on the side wall of the Boot Hill Saloon.

Right, from top: Bikers gather at the Cabbage Patch to drink beer, party and watch the coleslaw wrestlers; Boot Hill Saloon, an internationally known bikers' bar on Main Street; the view at the Iron Horse Saloon; thousands of bikers visit the Iron Horse Saloon every day during Bike Week.

Destination Daytona—the largest Harley-Davidson motorcycle dealer in the world.

Riding a motorcycle is a very different experience than driving a car. Motorcycling gives riders a sense of camaraderie with each other – and against vehicles with four or more wheels.

Other popular biker hangouts include Dirty Harry's, Froggy's Saloon, the Full Moon Saloon, the Highlander Cafe, Jackson Hole Saloon, Last Resort Bar, River Deck, Wild Bill's Saloon, Smiley's Tap, Bank & Blues Club, and Broken Spoke Saloon.

POPULAR BIKE RIDING PATHS

In addition to sport racing, bike shows, parades, and people watching, the Daytona Beach area offers many excellent riding roadways. For many bikers, it's the local scenery that makes repeated trips worthwhile. If bikers don't mind getting sand and salt spray onto their nice paint jobs, a ride down Daytona Beach's wide beach is interesting and informative of some of the history that made Bike Week possible. Many bikers ride along the surf and on inland roadways. U. S. Highway A1A from St. Augustine to the Ponce Inlet Lighthouse is one of the most beautiful motorcycle roadways in Florida. The Daytona Beach area has many inland off-the-beat roadways to New Smyrna Beach, Samsula, DeLand and Astor.

A driving pathway called the "Loop" is very popular with motorcycle enthusiasts. It is a bike rider's dream that offers open road, sunshine,

For many bikers, it is the local scenery that makes repeated trips worthwhile. The Daytona Beach area has many interesting biker roadways: the "Loop" in Ormond Beach, U. S. Highway A1A along the Atlantic Ocean between St. Augustine and Ormond Beach, State Road 11 through the orange groves north of DeLand, and U. S. Highway 17 from DeLand to Crescent City.

Most riders search for that secluded, less busy road that might enable them to ride in as much safety as is possible, albeit in an exciting way. The freeways that carry heavy truck traffic is not the best place for a motorcyclist. The motorcycle rider must rediscover old routes and old roads. Perhaps in a romantic way, the motorcyclist must turn back the pages of history, not to impassable and impossible roads but to less major and less modern ones.

and many graceful curves. The Loop, a twenty-two mile ride through real Florida countryside, starts on John Anderson Drive in Ormond Beach (north of Daytona Beach) at the Granada Bridge. Head north, along the Halifax River, to Highbridge Road, turn west and go over the Intercoastal Waterway (also called the Halifax River). Turn west on Walter Boardman Road, then south on the tree-lined Old Dixie Highway back toward Ormond Beach. Sights along the way include a 400-year-old Fairchild Oak, Ormond Park, and early sugar plantation ruins. The Loop is a must for bike riders who enjoy the open road and Florida's natural beauty.

Other popular biker roadways are State Road 11 from DeLand to Bunnell; U.S. Highway 17 from DeLand to Crescent City; and the two-lane road from Enterprise to Osteen, along Lake Monroe.

There is a lot more to motorcycling than simply riding a bike. Owning and using a motorcycle gives a different perspective than that of the average pedestrian or car driver. Depending on the rider, the machine, and the moment, you are an individual—free, rebellious, fast-moving, glamorous, maybe persecuted, even pitied, always vulnerable. Those shared emotions produce a bond between motorcyclists that can sometimes bridge the huge gaps between the many different types of riders.

DAYTONA SUPERCROSS

In 1971, a new form of competition, Supercross, was added to the races during Bike Week. The first Daytona Supercross course was constructed in an area of the Daytona International Speedway infield. The first race in the American Motorcycle Association Supercross Championship was held at Daytona Beach track.

The Supercross is one of the most exciting events during Bike Week. Racing "in any weather" means that if it happened to rain and the track was muddy, you would be lucky to even see the bike numbers after a few laps. The event has transformed into a serious, professional sport. Today's high-flying stars of motorcycle factory teams routinely perform aerial acrobatics and seventy-foot leaps.

The following lists some of the racers who have performed on the Daytona Supercross racecourse: Chad Reed, Ricky Carmichael, Jeremy McGrath, Mike Kiedrowski, Jeff Stanton, Rick Johnson, Bob Hannah and Jimmy Weinert.

Supercross rider.

BIKETOBERFEST

Biketoberfest is a smaller version of Bike Week held in Daytona Beach each October. The event started in 1992 with 5,000 visitors and, in 2001, the attendance swelled to over 100,000. Biketoberfest is a popular biker event that draws about one-fifth of the biker crowd that visits Daytona Beach in the spring. It is the Baby Brother of Bike Week.

Just like Bike Week, however, most bikers come to Biketoberfest to party. They come to enjoy the pungent aroma of exhaust pipes and food cooking on Main Street. They come to purchase a new Boot Hill Saloon T-shirt or to ride their bikes on the beach. But as usual, after all the beer has been consumed and the party is over, the bikers head for home, and Daytona Beach returns to normalcy. The quietness will remain for a few months until next year's Bike Week again attracts the biker crowd.

Viewing Biketoberfest from the air.

The Daytona Supercross track. Clip: A supercross bike.

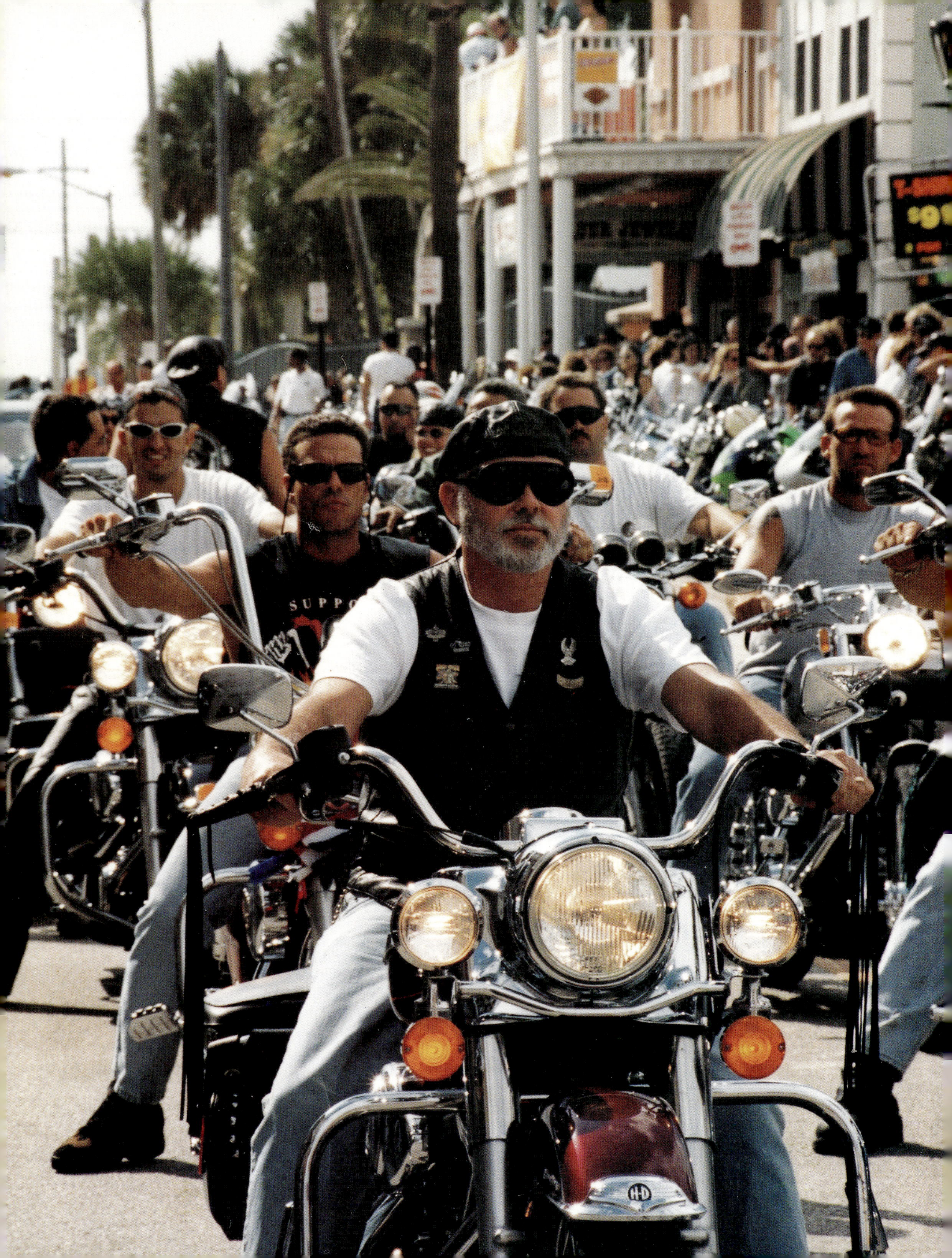
H-D

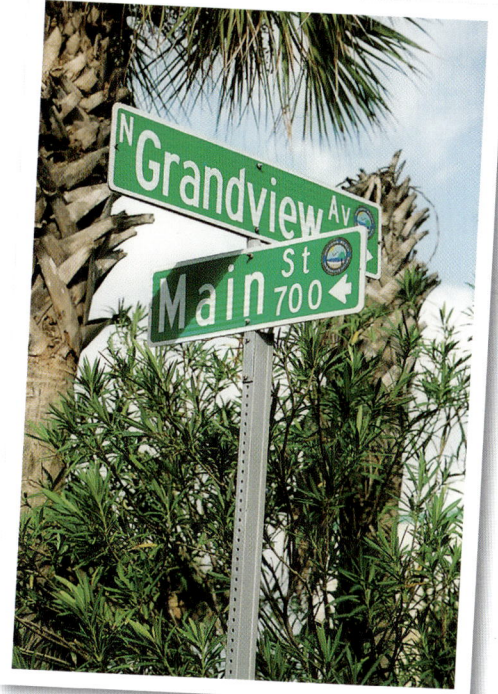

Main Street in Daytona Beach becomes a long thread of motorcycles as Bike Week celebrants do what they like to do—ride their bikes. During the 10-day event, Main Street becomes handlebar-to-handlebar with Harley-Davidson bikes and other two-wheelers. Bikers park their motorcycles on Main Street and then join thousands of other spectators watching customized Harley-Davidson bikes pass in front of them. People-watching is one of the most popular activities during Bike Week.

Spectators to Main Street bikers will see almost everything: Harleys of all shapes and hues; bejeweled custom bikes next to the most awful ratbike; bikes with massive V-8 car motors grafted in; vintage Indian bikes; old British motorcycles such as Ariels, Nortons and Triumphs; even oddballs such as Vincent V-twins and Velocette singles, plus countless one-of-a-kind special bikes of every size and description.

Most visitors to Bike Week enjoy riding their bikes on Main Street because they know that is where they will always have an audience.

A convoy of motorcycles makes its way east on Main Street in Daytona Beach. Thousands of bikes make this trip on Daytona's most popular biker roadway.

Daytona Beach viewing tower.

Checking out Main Street.

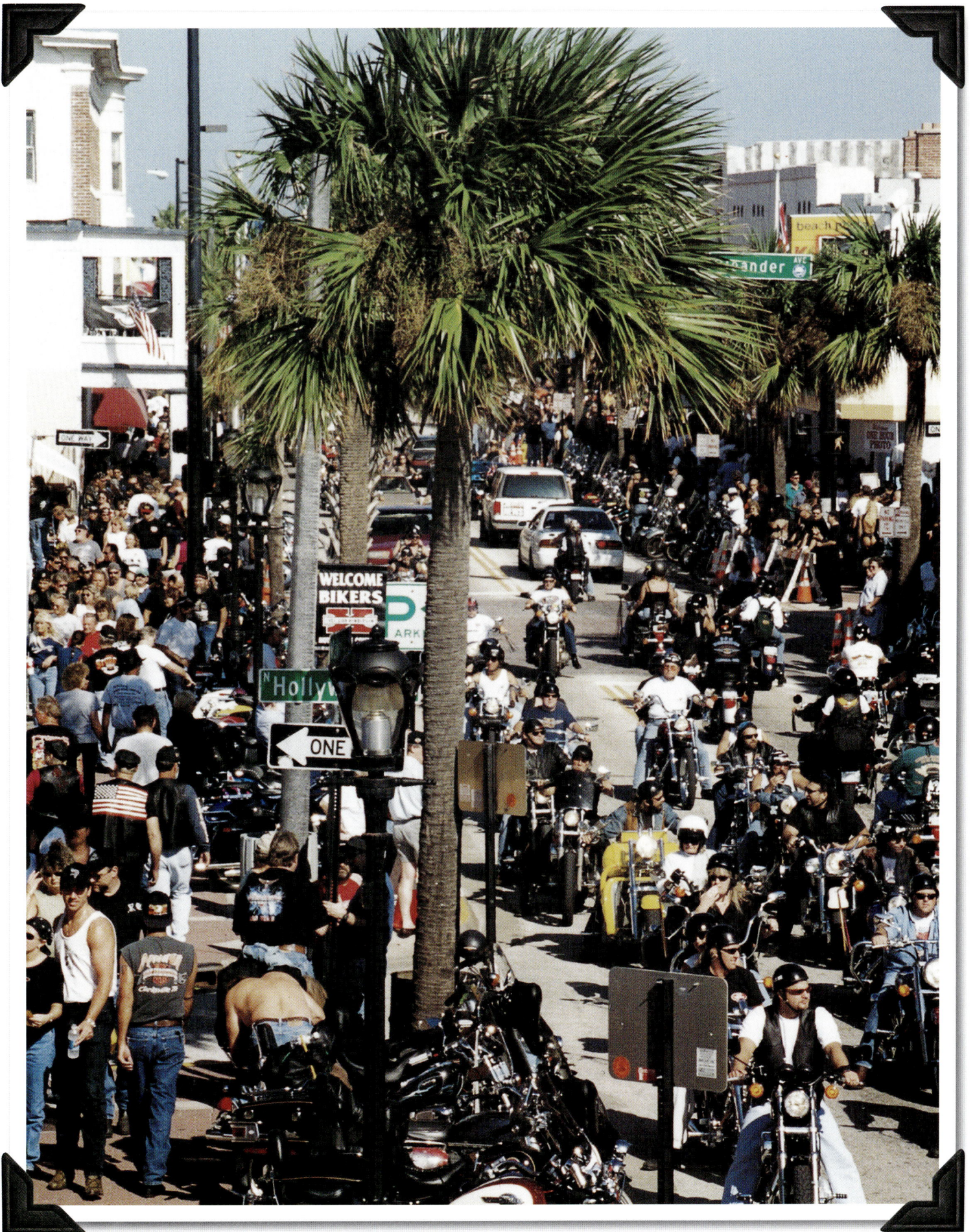

Bird's-eye view of Main Street traffic.

The most popular bike on Main Street—the Harley-Davidson. Some celebrity Harley-Davidson bike riders have included Elvis Presley, Clint Eastwood, Jay Leno, Dan Ackroyd, Cher, Whoopie Goldberg, Bob Dylan, Muhammad Ali, Sly Stallone, Malcolm Forbes, Roy Rogers and Peter Fonda. Interestingly, ten percent of Harley riders are female.

An unusual site—a bicycle!

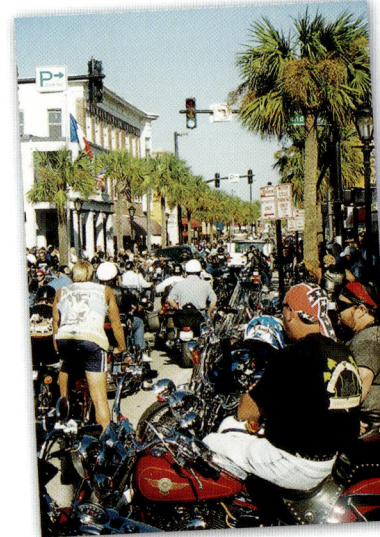

Even though many of the bikers look wild, the vast majority are well-behaved and courteous.

A Main Street traffic jam is a good time to get a closer look at great bikes that may have been passing by.

This biker is taking a break from Main Street activities.

Top: Sunny skies and palm trees greet Bike Week attendees. Below: The Boardwalk is located at the eastern end of Main Street.

An integral part of Bike Week, the Boardwalk has grown from a side event into a show in its own right. Custom bikes of all shapes, sizes and types can be seen there every year.

Motorcycle modeling on the Boardwalk.

The Budweiser Clydesdales marching on Main Street.

Bikers overlooking the Boardwalk and beach from a cable car.

This young lady is advertising the Biker Swap Meet at the Volusia County Fairgrounds in DeLand.

Getting ready for a bike show on the Boardwalk. Bikers take good care of their bikes, cleaning, polishing, inspecting...

Bank & Blues club on Main Street.

Entertainer on the Boardwalk.

Clockwise from top left: Bikers watching Main Street activities from the Upper Deck. A few of the 500,000 bikers who attended Bike Week 2000. The Pinewood Cemetery is across the street from the Boot Hill Saloon.

The Boot Hill Saloon on Main Street is a destination biker bar for many Bike Week attendees.

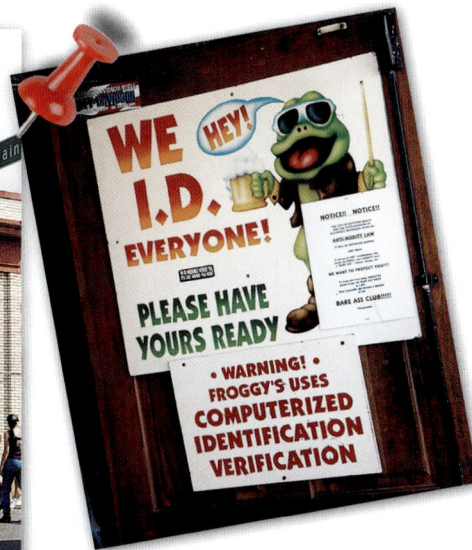

Froggy's Saloon on Main Street, and the front door sign.

Bike parking is always a problem near Main Street.

The Fernwood Hotel, located on the northeast corner of Wild Olive Avenue and Main Street, was demolished in 2001.

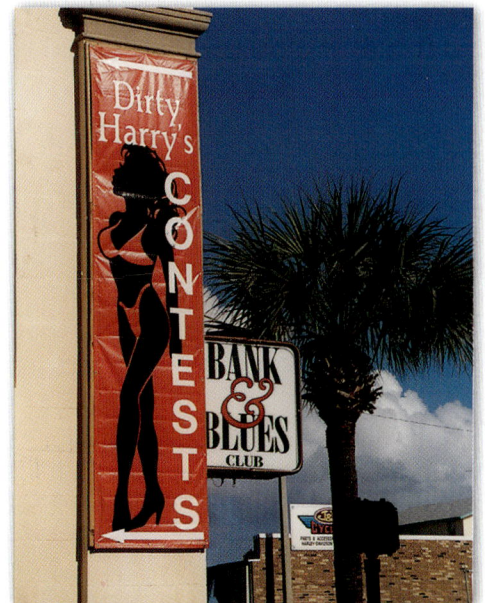

Main Street entertainment.

The Corbin building stands in the background as bikers pass by on their way to cross the Main Street bridge over the Halifax River. Corbin is now located on Nova Road.

NO
CLUB COLORS
ANIMALS
REPTILES, BIRDS, ETC.
(FROGS ALLOWED)
DRUGS
ATTITUDES
WEAPONS

No club colors.

Will Work FOR BEER

There was once a biker who decided to write a drinking song... but he could never get past the first few bars.

The Pinewood Cemetery.

Welcome to Bike Week!

These guys are probably discussing needlework.

Don't you believe it.

Everybody looks at the pretty girls.

A Main Street fashion statement

Clockwise from top left: Just two rules on Main Street: stay cool, and look mean. Don't be fooled; by Monday morning he will be back in suit and tie. And people say all motorcycle riders are alike... A pretty biker on Main Street. Furry passengers (even stuffed ones) are allowed during Bike Week. Taking a break from directing traffic. Exhibitionism is not hard to find during Bike Week; Shown here on Main Street is Bobby Yogerst. Let's hope one of the merchants sells him a new outfit.

Many bikers show their children—future bikers—the activities on Main Street.

Gilly's Pub 44 River Front, located just east of the Main Street Bridge, overlooks the beautiful Halifax River. Bikers enjoy sitting on the outdoor patio and watching the birds and boat traffic.

Spectators on the Upper Deck get a good view of Main Street action.

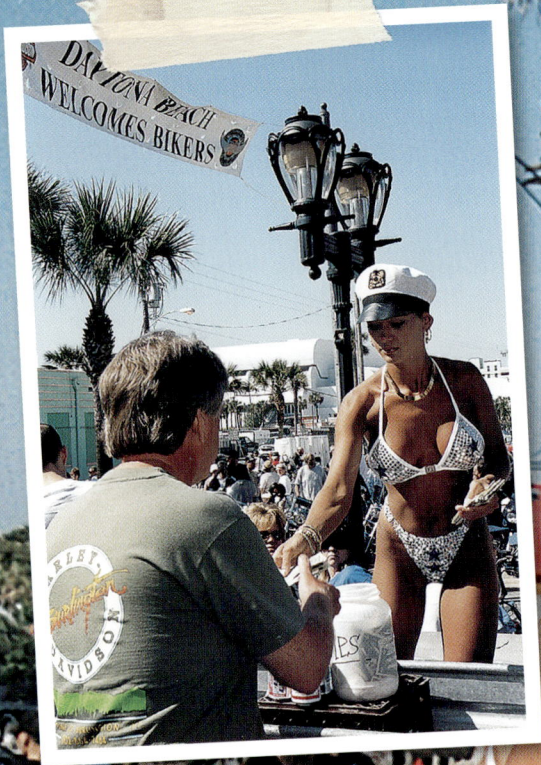

TIPS

CHAPTER 3
BEER BABES OF BIKE WEEK

The Beer Babe toils tirelessly, never complaining, opening can after cold can.

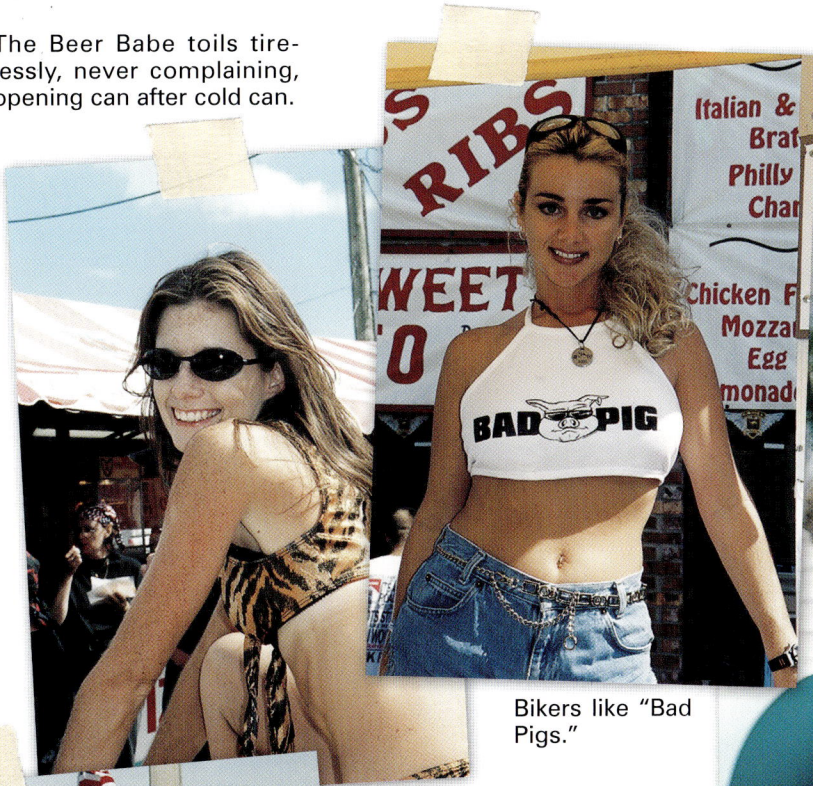

Bikers like "Bad Pigs."

Beer sales have been good today.

Another "Bad Pig."

Not an official biker outfit, but do you think the bikers complained?

I'll have a Budweiser!

I'll sell you all the beer you want.

Heather was also appearing in the current edition of Playboy magazine when this photo was taken during Bike Week 2006.

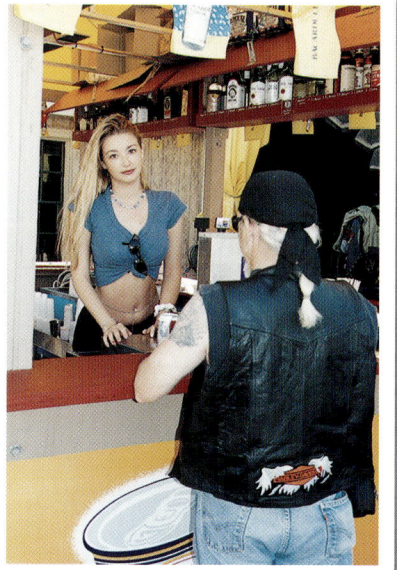

From top: Smile! Cool outfit. Pretty girls are everywhere.

I'm often called a "Suds Slinger."

Do you like my outfit?

Another pretty smile on Main Street.

Not another photographer!

Always has on a smile.

We work for tips only!!!

I sold more beer yesterday!

How do you like my new outfit?

Boy, I'm sure going to have a good story to tell my buddies when I get home!

Pretty smiles everywhere.

A dollar tip would be nice.

Smiling for the photographer.

I hope it doesn't rain!

I'll be with you in a minute.

Another beautiful Beer Babe.

Want another beer?

Will you tip me if I smile?

Do you like
my graphics?

Publicity photo for Buzz Co. in Chicago.

Are you next?

I don't take Canadian money!

A pretty smile at the Full Moon Saloon.

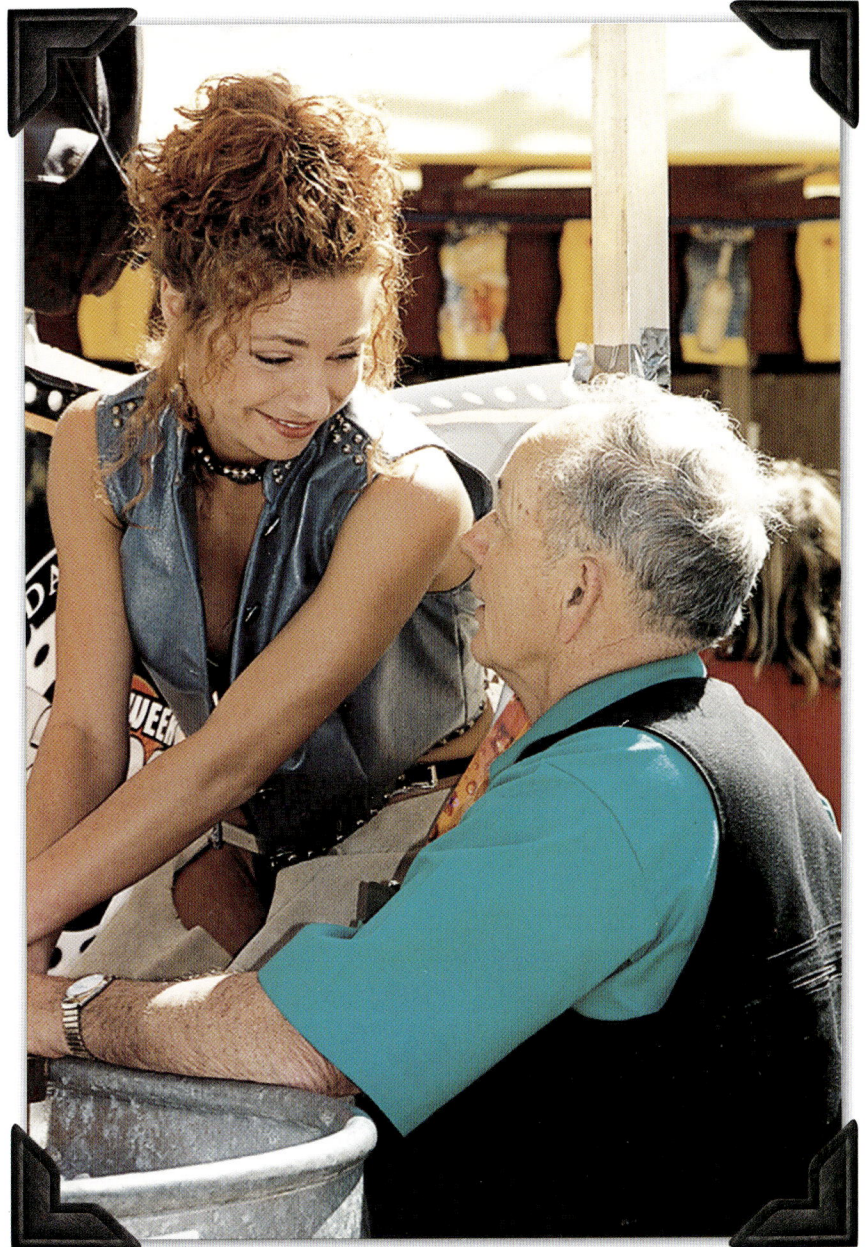

No, I don't remember you from last year.

Pay for the beer and move out of the way.

You better be 21 or older!

I don't care if you do have a Japanese bike – I don't have any Japanese beer.

49

Bikers are some of the funniest people I have ever met.

Proof that I've been to Bike Week.

I've got Budweiser, Coors and Miller.

The beads make the outfit.

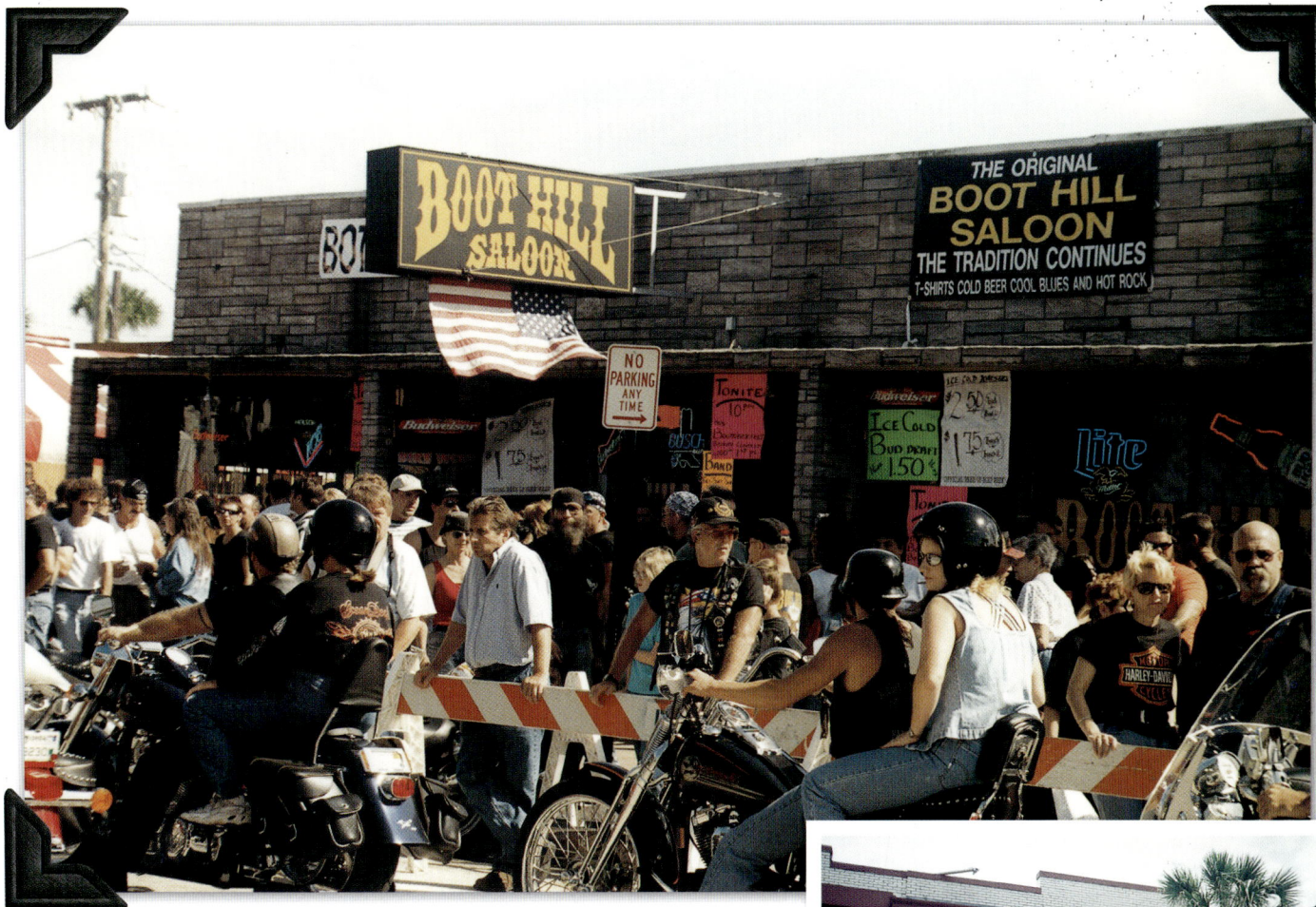

During Bike Week and Biketoberfest the Boot Hill Saloon on Main Street is often wall-to-wall with bikers as they stop by to enjoy a brew. While there, they often purchase a "Boot Hill" T-shirt to wear with pride while in town and to take back home. Decades of biker memorabilia line the walls of this popular biker bar. The Saloon's motto is "Order a drink and have a seat—You're better off here than across the street." (The old Pinewood Cemetery is located across the street.)

Froggy's Saloon is a popular Main Street biker handout.

Bikers flock to Dirty Harry's on Main Street to watch the wet T-Shirt contests.

DirtyHarry's
DAILY CONTESTS
WET T-SHIRTS
2:00 - 5:00 - 7:00 PM DAILY

3 HOT BANDS
DAYTIME · EVENING · LATE NIGHT

WET T-SHIRTS!

Wow! That ice water is cold.

Destination Daytona. During Bike Week thousands of Harley-Davidson motorcycle riders flock to this location to see the latest Harleys, visit vendors, enjoy the entertainment, and dine in one of the many eating establishments.

Spot the Yamaha bike in this Iron Horse Saloon scene.

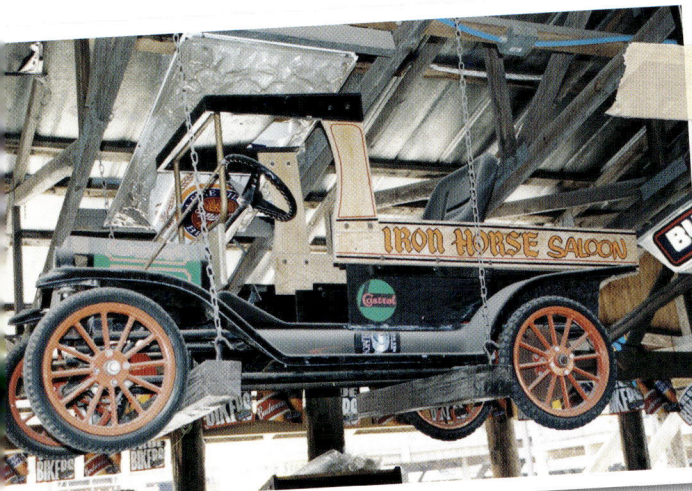

The Iron Horse Saloon contains several outdoor bars, a bandstand, food booths, vendor booths, a sprawling elevated boardwalk, a burn-out pit, a Wall of Death attraction and parking for many bikes.

Tire salesmen love these guys. This Burn-Out Pit is located at the Iron Horse Saloon.

Iron Horse Saloon bike.

IRON HORSE
SALOON
MPORTED
CIGARS
BIG PAPA
BAR-B-QUE
NO
PARKING
ANY
TIME

Wild Bill's Saloon on U. S. Highway 1 in Ormond Beach.

Smiley's Tap. What started innocently enough as cooking two hams has now become a monster pig roast. Located at 1161 North U. S. Highway 1 (just north of the Iron Horse Saloon), Smiley's Tap, a bikers' bar run by a female biker, specializes in pit-cooked pig and chicken, and homemade coleslaw. Bikers driving by smell the food and stop in. It is a popular spot during Bike Week.

The Bar-In-A-Tree at the Iron Horse Saloon.

Bike parking at the Iron Horse Saloon.

The entertainment stage at the Iron Horse Saloon.

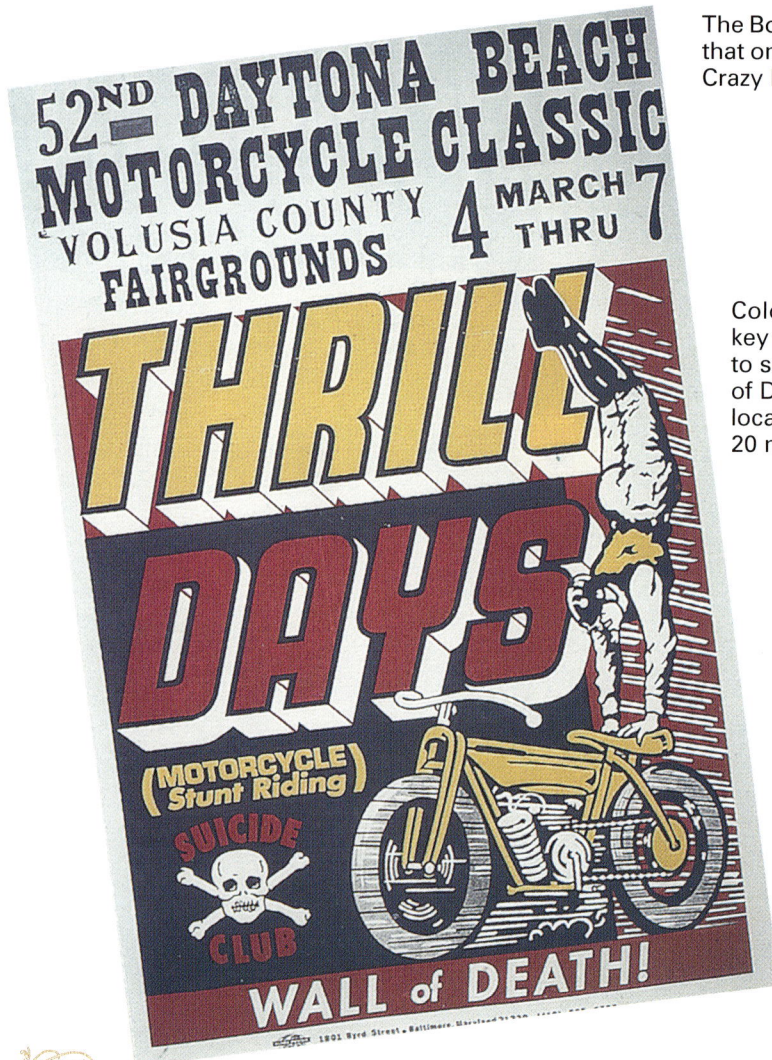

The Boot Hill Saloon II continues with the same biker activities that once appeared at the Jackson Hole Saloon, including the Crazy Bike Ride attraction.

Colorful, attractive posters are the key to luring bikers and other folks to see dare devil stunts and the Wall of Death riders. The Fairgrounds are located near DeLand, which is about 20 miles from Daytona Beach.

Next Wall of Death show is at 2 p.m. During the 1930s, Roland "Rollie" Free and O. K. Newby performed in a Wall of Death ride where a lion was turned loose in the barrel to take swipes at the rider as he circled the top of the barrel at great speed.

The Wall of Death is an all-American marriage of motorcycles, P. T. Barnum-style showmanship, and death-defying daredevilry. This stunt-riding attraction uses a barrel-like chamber with high walls that create a never-ending vertical road, and a daredevil motorcycle rider that drives the bike around the inside at top speed. There are many variations, using sidecars, lion cubs, riding in opposite directions, hands-off riding, sitting backward, and all manner of stunts. For decades bikers attending Bike Week and Biketoberfest have anted up their hard-earned cash to be dazzled by the spectacle and deafened by the contained roar of the cycle. Most Wall of Death riders use lightweight Indian Scout motorcycles, however, a few riders have preferred to use lightweight Japanese made cycles. The Indian motorcycle is balanced, nearly vibrationless, and performs well in all types of stunt riding. The above photograph was taken at the Iron Horse Saloon during Bike Week.

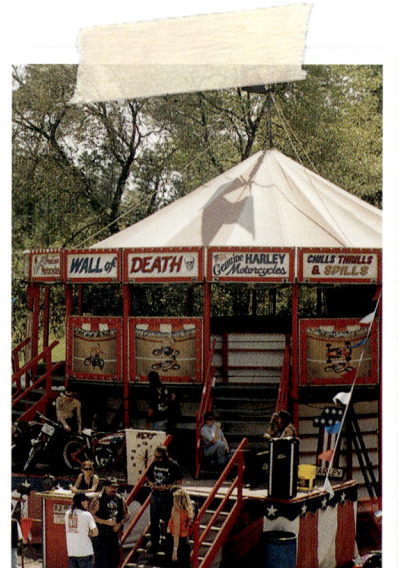

Wall of Death stunt riding attraction during Biketoberfest 1998.

This group of Bike Week visitors are entering the Wall of Death at the Iron Horse Saloon. They are about to witness a thrilling performance by Indian motorcycle riders.

This rider is demonstrating the Indian Scout motorcycle, which was lightweight yet perfectly balanced. It was the ideal bike for thrilling Wall of Death performances.

The entertainment stage at the Hog Pen in
Ormond Beach.

Park your bike and have
a beer at Jackson Hole.
This popular biker bar
later became the Boot
Hill Saloon II.

The Highlander Cafe in South Daytona.

The Last Resort Bar, located on U. S. Highway 1 south of Daytona Beach, is a popular biker hangout during Bike Week. This photograph shows a row of bikes along U. S. Highway 1 in front of the small bar. Several activities are located in a lot behind the bar.

Gilly's Pub 44 in New Smyrna Beach always draws a large crowd during biking events.

The Harley-Davidson Shop in New Smyrna Beach, just south of Daytona Beach. The shop is located next to Gilly's Pub 44.

The Harley-Davidson Shop in downtown Daytona Beach is the Beach Street center of biker activities during Bike Week and Biketoberfest.

At one time this WAS the largest Harley-Davidson Shop in the world, however, the largest shop now is located at Destination Daytona, north of Daytona Beach. Both shops have the same owner.

Carl's Speed Shop on Beach Street, now located on Nova Road.

The Riverfront Park vendor area on Beach Street.

Hawaiian Tropic models welcoming bikers to vendor booths.

Riding among the palm trees on Beach Street in downtown Daytona Beach.

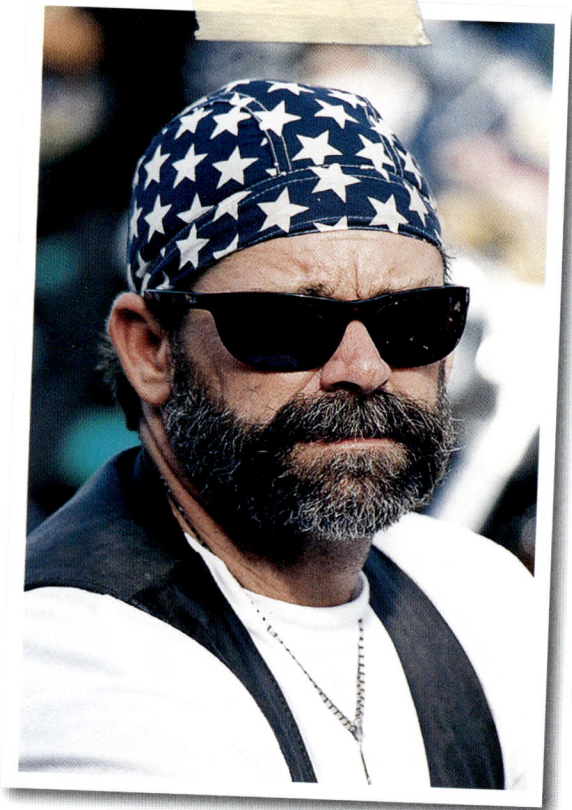

Hurry up and take the picture.

The Budweiser Clydesdales marching on Beach Street.

This is the way to view motorcycle events during Bike Week.

Believe it or not, this pretty girl is *selling* custom bikes on Beach Street.

HOG'S BREATH
BEER
HARLEY-DAVIDSON
ASS, GAS OR GRASS
NOBODY RIDES FOR FREE!
CAPT. STICKY
The
LAST RESORT
Bar
Bike Week

CHAPTER 6

U. S. HIGHWAY 1 BIKER SPOTS

Several popular Bike Week biker hangouts are scattered along U. S. Highway 1 from Ormond Beach North, south to Edgewater, including Destination Daytona, Smiley's Tap, Broken Spoke Saloon, Wild Bill's Saloon, Jackson Hole Saloon, Boot Hill Saloon II, Hog Pen, Iron Horse Saloon, The Station, Tropical Tattoo, Highlander Cafe, River Deck, Black Hills Saloon, Last Resort Bar, and No Name Saloon.

The party grows bigger every year. The biker attractions along U. S. Highway 1 are ground zero for a great time. Lots of good music, cold beer, delicious food, interesting entertainment, and incredible bikes.

I've got a match here somewhere...

Bruce Rossmeyer's Destination Daytona, located at 1637 North U. S. Highway 1 is the world's largest Harley-Davidson motorcycle dealer. During Bike Week, this 150-acre facility comes alive with thousands of biker enthusiasts visiting the 109,000-square-foot motorcycle showroom and surrounding activities. Entertainment includes live bands, bikini contests, T-Shirt give-away events, and a Wall of Death Stunt riding attraction. The surrounding area includes a hotel, motels, restaurants, specialty shops, motorcycle vendors, pubs, and food booths. During 2006, 2007, and 2008, many of the biker related events that once appeared at Beach Street locations, moved to the Destination Daytona area.

A biker crowd surrounding the Harley-Davidson motorcycle showroom.

The Harley-Davidson motorcycle showroom is a large, two-story display of motorcycles and related accessories.

A traveling Wall of Death stunt attraction, set up in the Destination Daytona area.

Smiley's Tap, located at 11161 North U. S. Highway 1, is a popular watering hole that offers bikers nightly bonfires, music, contests, barbeque, and motorcycle vendor booths.

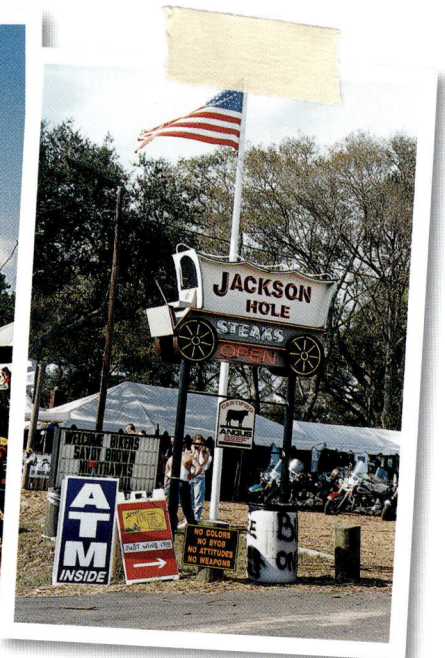

For many years the Jackson Hole Saloon was a popular biker hangout with attractions, vendors, nightly entertainment, and bon fires. In 2005 the name was changed to Boot Hill Saloon ll.

Eat, drink, and have fun.

Next stop, Sturgis—1,972 miles.

Anyone want another beer?

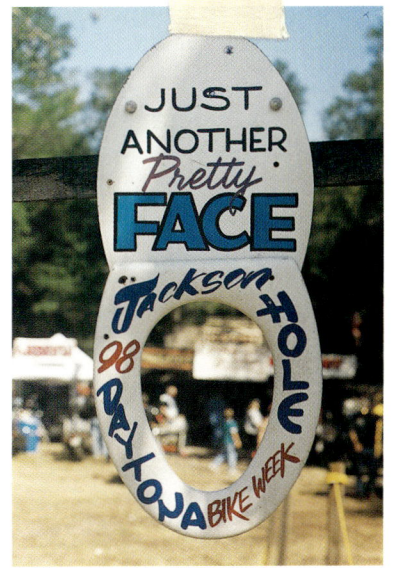

A Jackson Hole Saloon picture frame.

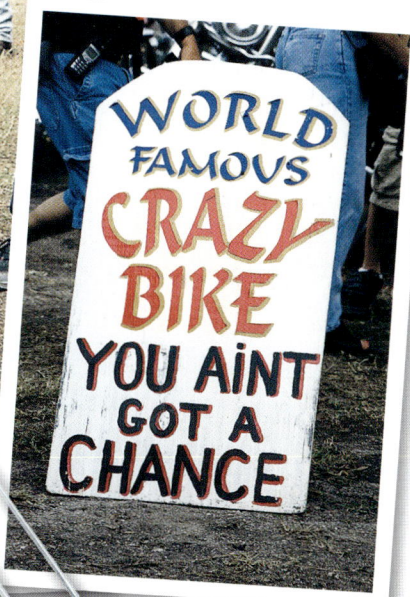

Try riding this small bike at Jackson Hole Saloon's "Crazy Bike" attraction! The only person that this author has seen ride the bike is the owner of the attraction.

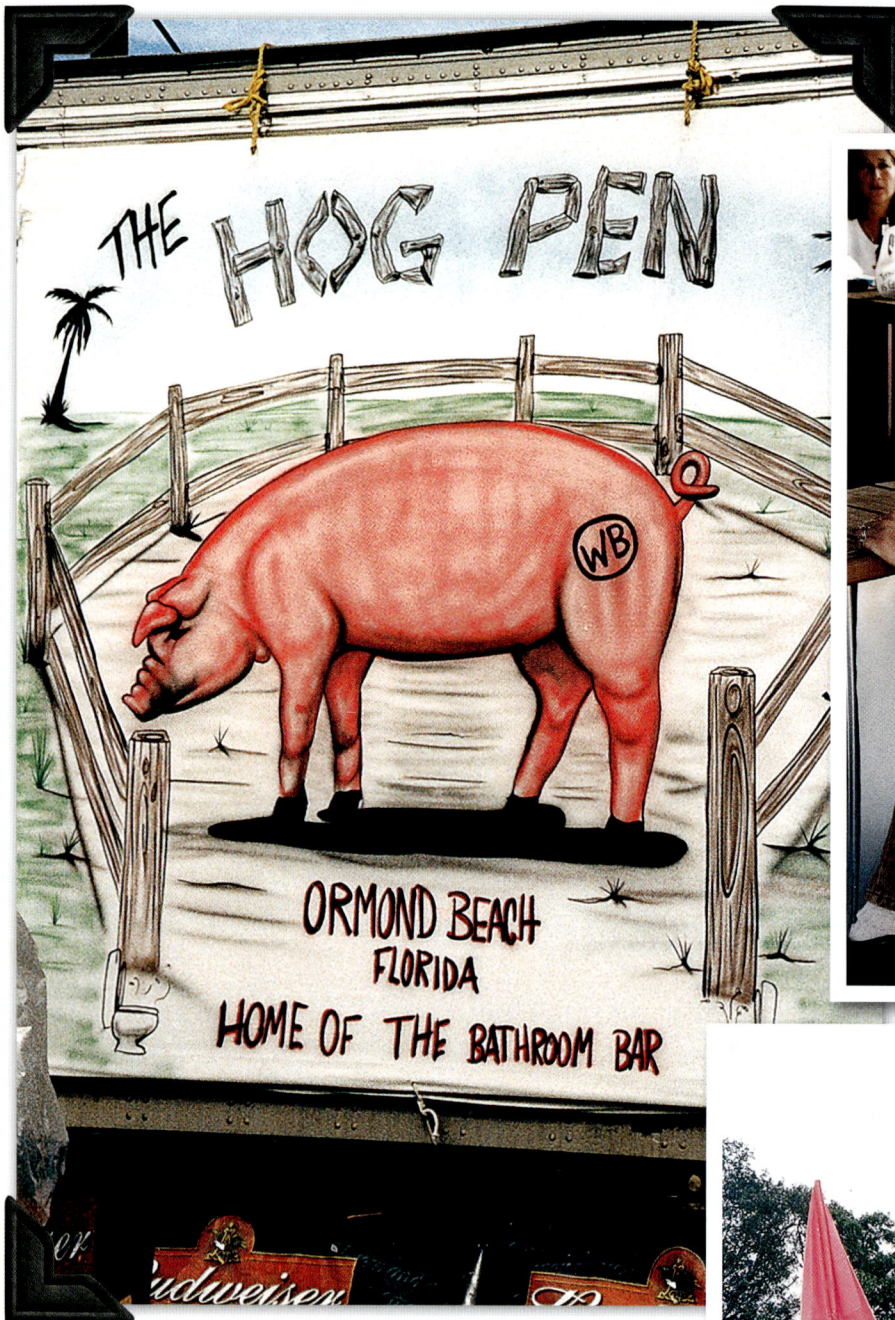

THE HOG PEN

ORMOND BEACH
FLORIDA
HOME OF THE BATHROOM BAR

This lady biker is enjoying the Bathroom Bar at the Hog Pen.

The Hog Pen, home of the Bathroom Bar, is located on U. S. Highway 1 in Ormond Beach.

King Hog throne at the Hog Pen.

This handmade sign on U. S. Highway 1 in Ormond Beach directed bikers to Iron Horse Saloon, Jackson Hole Saloon (now Boot Hill Saloon II), and Wild Bill's Saloon.

Wild Bill's Saloon has a collection of wooden motorcycles on display.

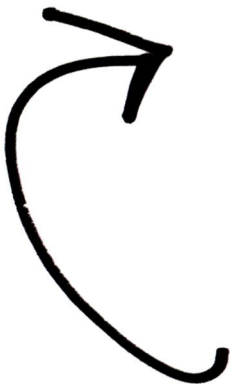

Bikers congregating in South Daytona.

Black Hills Saloon is a small tavern on U. S. Highway 1, south of Daytona Beach between South Daytona and the Last Resort Bar. Bikers enjoy the outside bar and lots of parking.

The Last Resort Bar, located on U. S. Highway 1 south of Daytona Beach, draws thousands of visiting bikers during Bike Week. This rustic watering hole has contests, entertainment, an interesting environment, motorcycle vendors, lots of food, and cold beer.

Gilly's

PUB

44

STEAKS · BURGERS

WELCOME
BIKE WEEK
2000

CHAPTER 7

AROUND DAYTONA BEACH

Daytona Beach is surrounded by many bars and facilities that attract visiting bikers during Bike Week, such as the Harley-Davidson motorcycle shop and Gilly's Pub 44 in New Smyrna Beach; Sopotnick's Cabbage Patch at 549 Tomoka Farms Road in Samsula; Crazy Girls, Custom Iron, and OB's Lounge in DeLand; and Finnegan's Pub and High Tides "Snack Jack" in Flagler Beach.

Shown above is the Harley-Davidson Shop in New Smyrna Beach, located next door to Gilly's Pub 44.

Palm trees, cold beer, lovely weather, visiting bikers, and Gilly's Pub 44: a Bike Week tradition.

Gilly's Pub 44, located in New Smyrna Beach, attracts visiting bikers during Bike Week like Walt Disney World in Orlando attracts children.

Bikers enjoying the Florida sun at Gilly's Pub 44 outdoor bar.

Party time at Gilly's Pub 44.

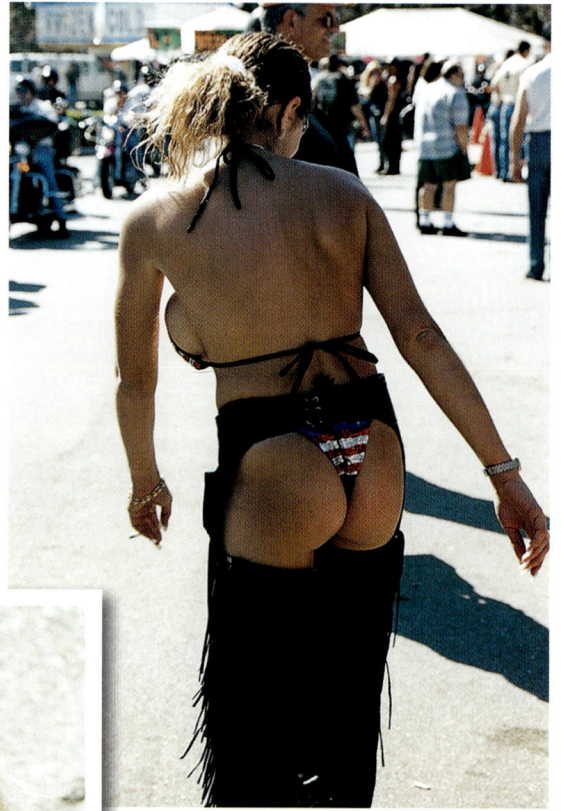

Scantily clad women tend to draw a crowd; hope these women don't get sunburned.

The famed Budweiser Clydesdales pull a brewery wagon at a Bike Week event at Sopotnick's Cabbage Patch in Samsula, a few miles from Daytona Beach. These attractive horses are always VIP guests at any biker gathering. Other attractions at the Cabbage Patch include a Coleslaw Wrestling Contest, Parachute Jumps, unusual bike exhibits, and vendors selling everything from helmets to black leather jackets, and, of course, hot dogs and beer. Several thousand bikers are often present to witness the wild and crazy Coleslaw Wrestling events.

A Cabbage Patch refueling station.

Fun and games at the Cabbage Patch.

Are we having fun yet?

Free Willi singing his heart out at the Cabbage Patch, shown with his ratbike.

This Cabbage Patch visitor is putting on her own show.

There are always large biker crowds watching the Coleslaw Wrestling Contests at the Cabbage Patch.

Budweiser Clydesdales parading on Main Street. It is always a wonderful treat to see the magnificent Clydesdale horses "up close and personal." Motorcycle noise does not seem to bother the horses. These huge horses are the stars of the parade.

CHAPTER 8
BIKER PARADES

Sampling the great outdoors on a motorcycle is more enjoyable when riders can share it with friends.

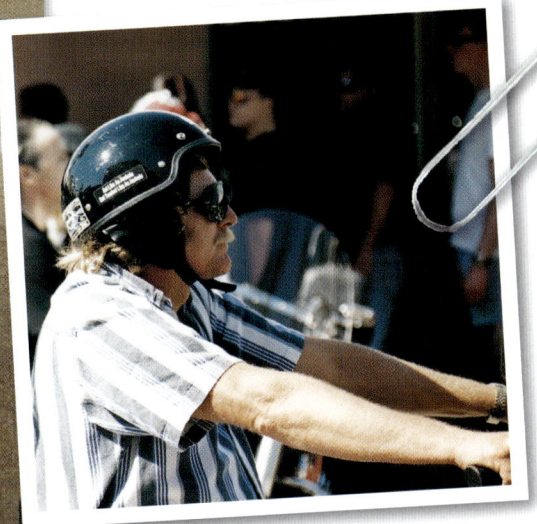

Color, camaraderie and excitement are all part of a parade, such as this one in Daytona Beach. Parades also offer the closest form of formation riding.

On the morning of the Daytona 200 Race, a parade runs from North U.S. Highway A1A west on Main Street and to the Daytona International Speedway. Most of the riders are driving Harley-Davidson bikes. There is a variety of other biker parades in the Daytona Beach area during Bike Week and Biketoberfest.

Where did everybody go?

Where's the party at?

Quit back-seat driving!

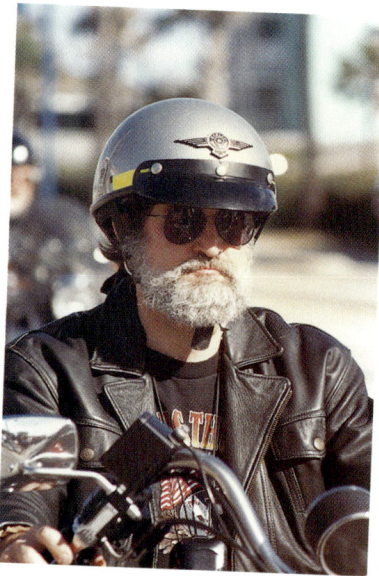
This is a long parade.

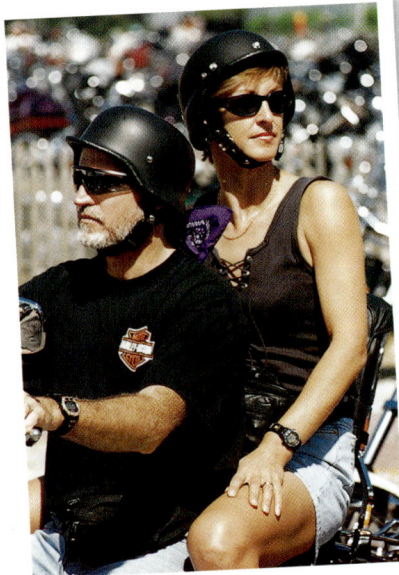
Part of a parade on U. S. Hwy A1A.

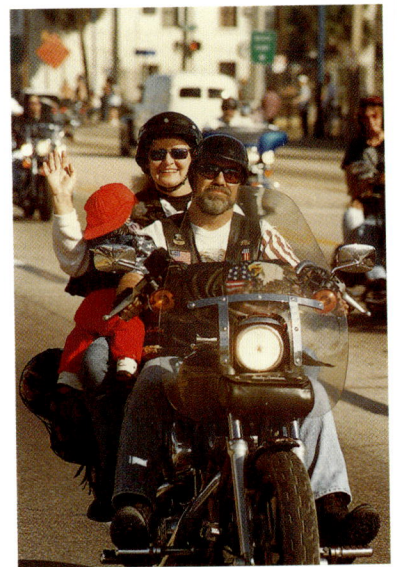
Out for a quiet Sunday ride.

Enjoying the parade.

"Father and son—fun for all ages."

And doggy makes three.

What a great life!

I ride a bike because its the only thing left the government can't control.

Strutting his stuff on Main Street.

Smile for the camera.

It's a miracle we all don't get run over.

Entertainment either by live bands or singers is a big part of Bike Week.

During the 1920s and '30s the beach racecourse at Daytona Beach witnessed a number of speed record attempts as men such as Sir Henry Seagrave and Malcolm Campbell fought for the glory of the world's fastest on four wheels, powering their British-built racecars along Daytona Beach's thin strip of silver sand. But soon the record breakers departed, forced out when speeds proved simply too great for such a narrow course. But this made space for another form of motor sport— the Daytona 200 motorcycle race.

The first Daytona 200 race was run in 1937, but Daytona Beach has been the home of gasoline speedsters since the beginning of the 20th century. At that time the sprawling Ormond Hotel was a popular haunt for wealthy northern industrialists, racecar owners, and racecar drivers who traveled south to enjoy the clear blue skies and sunny days of Florida. Amongst these men were Ransom E. Olds, founder of Oldsmobile; Alexander Winton, pioneer auto manufacturer; J. F. Hathaway, racing promoter; William J. Morgan, racing promoter; William K. Vanderbilt, Jr., playboy racecar driver; Barney Oldfield, racecar driver; Henry Ford, auto manufacturer; Walter Christie, racecar owner; Louis Chevrolet, auto manufacturer; Glenn Curtiss, motorcycle manufacturer; Fred Marriott, Stanley Steamer driver; Oscar Hedstrom, motorcycle manufacturer; Ralph de Palma, racecar

The first running of the Daytona 200 took place on January 24, 1937 on a 3.2 mile beach/road course located in the southern part of Daytona Beach.

In 1951 the rumble of Indian, Harley-Davidson, Triumph, BSA, and Norton motorcycles entering the North Turn of the Daytona Beach beach/road course drowned out the sound of the ocean waves and the yelling crowd. This view shows some of the Daytona 200 action.

The Daytona 200 race draws both entries and fans from many countries.

driver; Walter Christie, racecar manufacturer; Malcolm Campbell, racecar driver; and Sir Henry Segrave, racecar driver.

One of the first drivers to help establish racing records was Glenn Curtiss who built a V-8 motorcycle which (although never officially recorded) achieved over 136 MPH on the Ormond-Daytona Beach racecourse in 1907.

Most riders who have been involved in motorcycle roadracing, from the big international stars to the local privateers, have shared a similar dream to "Win Daytona." While there are a lot of other races and championships, no other event carries the prestige of the Daytona 200. It is the ultimate race to win.

Since 1937, a Daytona 200 victory has been the springboard of many great motorcycle racing careers. Top motorcycle legends, from early beach racing stars like Ed Kretz Sr., Benny Campanale, Dick Klamforth, and Brad Andres to modern day speedway superstars like Kenny Roberts, Scott Russell, Nicky Hayden, Matthew Mladin, and Miguel Duhamel all made their mark there.

Over the years, the Daytona 200 has had many different faces. It started out on the sandy beach racecourse south of Daytona Beach and since 1961 on the steep, banked turns of the Daytona International Speed-

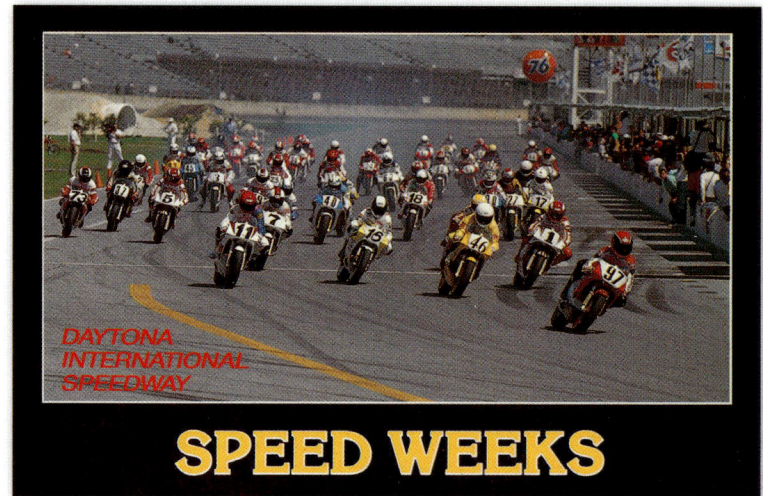

A cloud of smoke and the deafening roar of powerful engines heralds the start of the Daytona 200. Although the Daytona 200 race does not form part of the World Championship, it is probably the most prestigious single Superbike race in the world. On the banked track machines can achieve impressive speeds. The race takes place in March and traditionally heralds the start of the international racing season.

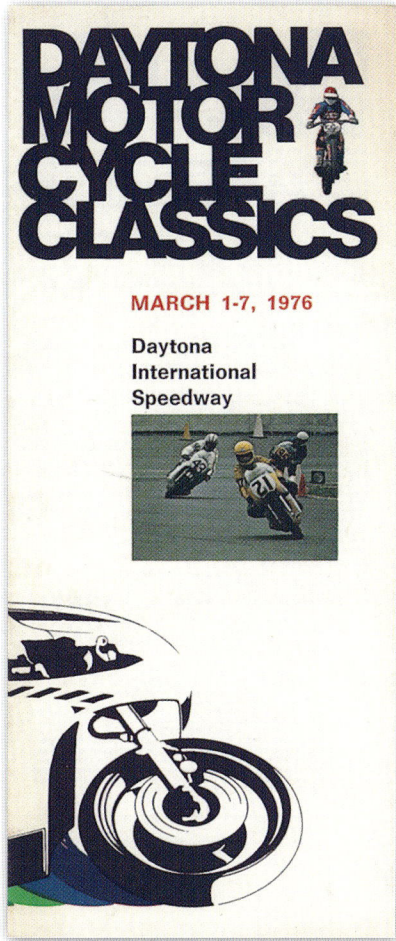

DAYTONA MOTOR CYCLE CLASSICS

MARCH 1-7, 1976

Daytona
International
Speedway

The 1976 Daytona International Speedway brochure that described the Daytona Motorcycle Classic races for the March 1976 event.

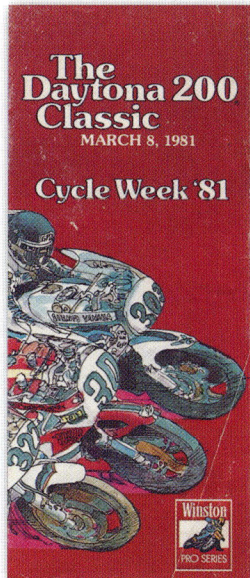

1981 Daytona Classic brochure.

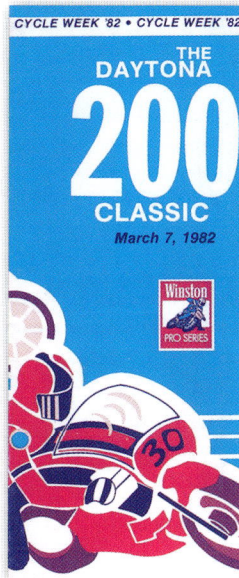

1982 Daytona 200 Classic brochure.

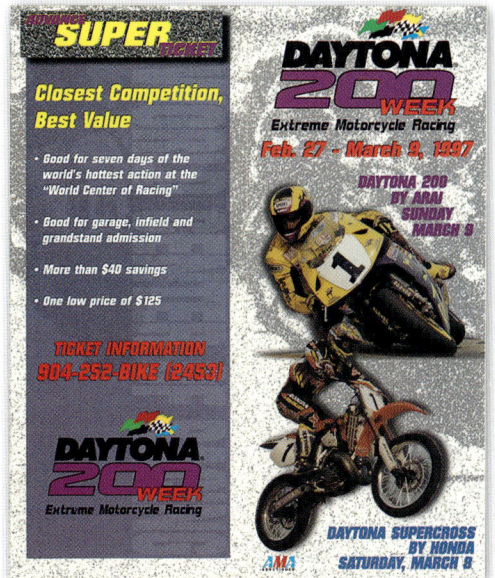

1997 Daytona 200 Motorcycle Race brochure.

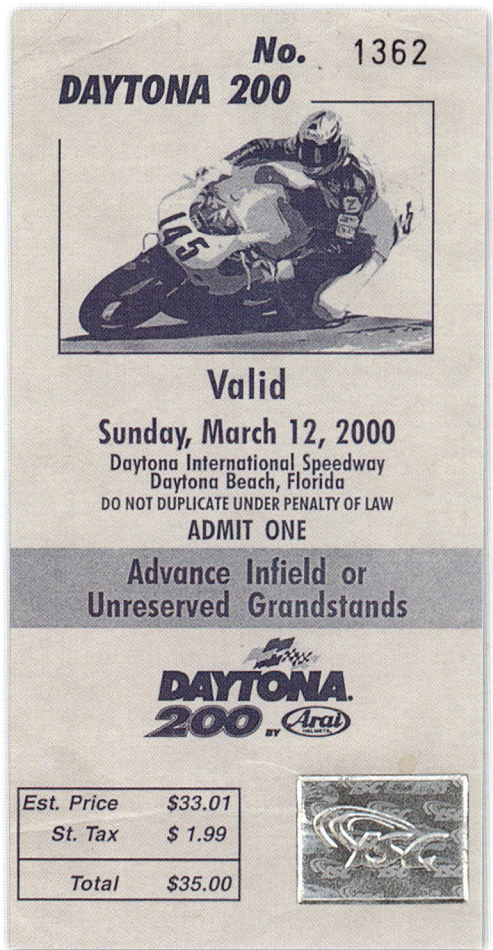

2000 Daytona 200 Motorcycle Race brochure.

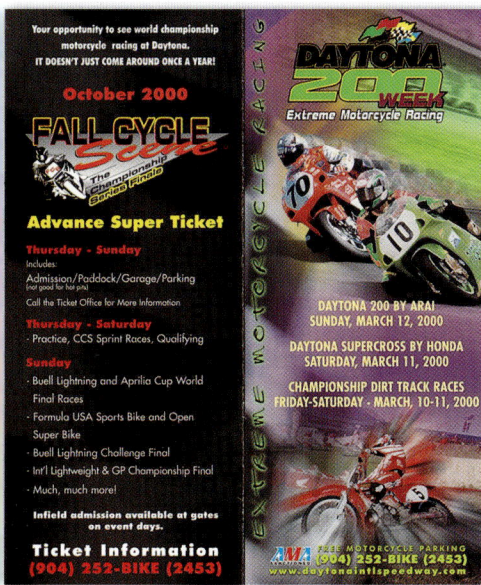

2002 Daytona 200 Motorcycle Race brochure.

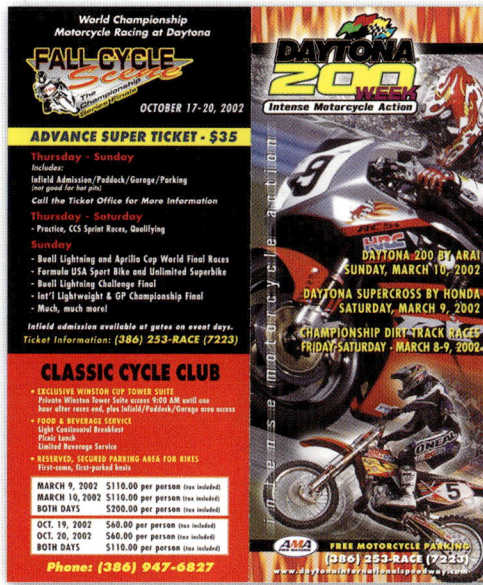

Daytona 200 Motorcycle Race ticket.

way. The motorcycles have also changed over the years as the sport has evolved. The Daytona 200 has seen every type of motorcycle, from the very simplistic to some of the most exotic.

THE BEACH-ROAD RACECOURSE

The beach-and-road racecourse where the Daytona 200 races were held from 1937 to 1961 was a track in no-man's-land in the thick, palmetto-covered sand dunes near Ponce DeLeon Inlet south of Daytona Beach. With half designed by nature, the beach and road track stood alone in international racing competition, a raceway man could not duplicate at any cost.

It was wild and dangerous and electrifying to watch the hot shoe experts broadside into the North turn connecting the beach with the road (U. S. Highway A1A), salt spray biting into their goggles and a rooster tail of sand flying in the wake of the racing machines and, of course, giving the oncoming riders a sand bath.

Riders raced northward on the beach and switched over to the road through an 180-degree turn built out of packed gravel and banked steeply through the sand dunes. Then the riders whizzed southward over a narrow, corrugated asphalt road (U. S. Highway A1A). Another 180-degree turn though the dunes at the South end of the road run dispatched the riders back to the beach. What an exciting racecourse it was.

Progress cut down the historic beach-road racecourse and made way for the Daytona International Speedway. Fickle ocean tides, a growing population in the Ponce Inlet area, and other factors doomed the beach-road raceway, and there will never be another to equal it.

The fastest Daytona 200 race on the beach-road racecourse was a rapid 99.86 MPH by Californian Joe

TABLE 1

YEAR	DRIVER	MOTORCYCLE TYPE	RACE TIME (MPH)
1937	Ed Kretz, Sr.	Indian	74.10
1938	Benny Campanale	Harley-Davidson	74.90
1939	Benny Campanale	Harley-Davidson	76.68
1940	Babe Tancrede	Harley-Davidson	75.11
1941	Billy Mathews	Norton	78.08
World War II: No Races			
1947	Johnny Spiegelhoff	Indian	77.14
1948	Floyd Emde	Indian	84.01
1949	Dick Klamfoth	Norton	86.42
1950	Billy Mathews	Norton	88.55
1951	Dick Klamfoth	Norton	92.81
1952	Dick Klamfoth	Norton	87.77
1953	Paul Goldsmith	Harley-Davidson	94.45
1954	Bobby Hill	BSA	94.24
1955	Brad Andres	Harley-Davidson	94.57
1956	Johnny Gibson	Harley-Davidson	94.21
1957	Joe Leonard	Harley-Davidson	98.52
1958	Joe Leonard	Harley-Davidson	99.86
1959	Brad Andres	Harley-Davidson	98.70
1960	Brad Andres	Harley-Davidson	98.06

Leonard in 1958. He was riding a Harley-Davidson motorcycle. It was ten years before this Daytona 200 speed record was topped at the Daytona International Speedway by Calvin Rayborn's 101.29 MPH ride on a Harley-Davidson.

The beach-road racecourse drivers, motorcycle type and race times are shown in Table 1.

THE DAYTONA INTERNATIONAL SPEEDWAY

The new site of the Daytona 200 motorcycle race was the Daytona International Speedway, a large concrete speedbowl with a trioval-shaped racetrack. The facility was built by race promoter Bill France as a showcase for such thrilling stock car races as the Daytona 500. In addition to the 2.5-mile trioval, with its three steeply banked turns and its prominent dip in the front stretch, the speedway has a long

winding course in its infield. This infield course was designed especially for motorcycle races, and, beginning in 1961, it was used along with the trioval for the Daytona 200, permanently replacing the old beach-road racecourse.

The move to the speedway thrust American motorcycle riders into the world of international competition, for Daytona's speedway attracted top European professional motorcyclists.

Riders on Harley-Davidson motorcycles won the Daytona 200 every year from 1961 to 1965. The factory-supported rider responsible for three of these Harley-Davidson victories was Roger Reiman of Illinois, who was Daytona's champion in 1961, 1964 and 1965.

The crowds at the speedway began to grow rapidly over the next few years. A record-breaking crowd of

35,000 turned out in 1968, when Calvin Rayborn of San Diego, California, scored his first Daytona 200 victory. Rayborn won the race again in 1969. Calvin Rayborn was the first rider at the Daytona speedway to average more than 100 MPH for the 200-mile race.

The 1970s was a decade of still more firsts at the Daytona International Speedway. In 1972 Don Emde became the first rider to win the Daytona 200 aboard a motorcycle powered by a two-stroke engine. Don Emde's father, Floyd, had won the Daytona 200 back in 1948 on the old beach-road racecourse. With Don's victory in 1972, Floyd and Don Emde became the first father-and-son combination to win the Daytona 200.

Riders who have won the Daytona 200 three or more times are Miguel Duhamel, 5 (1991, 1996, 1999, 2003, 2005); Scott Russel, 5 (1992, 1994, 1995, 1997, 1998); Matthew Mladin, 3 (2000, 2001, 2004); Kenny Roberts, 3 (1978, 1983, 1984); Roger Reiman, 3 (1961, 1964, 1965); and Brad Andres, 3 (1955, 1959, 1960).

The drivers, motorcycle type, and race times for Daytona 200 races at the Daytona International Speedway are shown in Table 2.

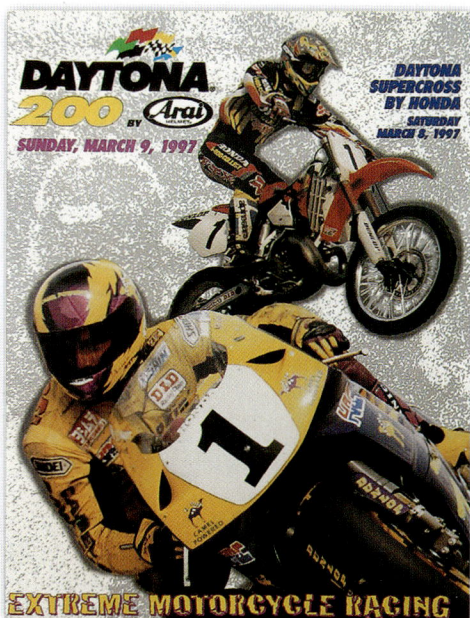

1997 Daytona 200 race program.

TABLE 2

YEAR	DRIVER	MOTORCYCLE TYPE	RACE TIME (MPH)
1961	Roger Reiman	Harley-Davidson	69.25
1962	Don Burnett	Triumph	71.99
1963	Ralph White	Harley-Davidson	77.68
1964	Roger Reiman	Harley-Davidson	94.83
1965	Roger Reiman	Harley-Davidson	90.04
1966	Buddy Elmore	Triumph	96.58
1967	Gary Nixon	Triumph	98.23
1968	Calvin Rayborn	Harley-Davidson	101.29
1969	Calvin Rayborn	Harley-Davidson	100.88
1970	Dick Mann	Honda	102.69
1971	Dick Mann	BSA	104.74
1972	Don Emde	Yamaha	103.36
1973	Jarno Saarinen	Yamaha	98.18
1974	Giacoma Agostini	Yamaha	105.01
1975	Gene Romero	Yamaha	106.45
1976	Johnny Cecotto	Yamaha	108.77
1977	Steve Baker	Yamaha	108.85
1978	Kenny Roberts	Yamaha	108.37
1979	Dale Singleton	Yamaha	107.69
1980	Patrick Pons	Yamaha	107.56
1981	Dale Singleton	Yamaha	108.52
1982	Graeme Crosby	Yamaha	109.10
1983	Kenny Roberts	Yamaha	110.93
1984	Kenny Roberts	Yamaha	113.14
1985	Freddie Spencer	Honda	102.99
1986	Eddie Lawson	Yamaha	106.03
1987	Wayne Rainey	Honda	106.83
1988	Kevin Schwantz	Suzuki	107.80
1989	John Ashmead	Honda	96.32
1990	David Sadowski	Yamaha	98.38
1991	Miguel Duhamel	Honda	93.47
1992	Scott Russell	Kawasaki	110.67
1993	Eddie Lawson	Yamaha	105.94
1994	Scott Russell	Kawasaki	85.01
1995	Scott Russell	Kawasaki	107.85
1996	Miguel Duhamel	Honda	108.82
1997	Scott Russell	Yamaha	105.87
1998	Scott Russell	Yamaha	111.78
1999	Miguel Duhamel	Honda	113.47
2000	Matthew Mladin	Suzuki	113.63
2001	Matthew Mladin	Suzuki	-
2002	Nicky Hayden	Honda	93.03
2003	Miguel Duhamel	Honda	113.83
2004	Matthew Mladin	Suzuki	113.90
2005	Miguel Duhamel	Honda	100.70
2006	Jake Zemke	Honda	100.28
2007	Steve Rapp	Kawasaki	101.65
2008	Chaz Davies	Kawasaki	98.80

Superbikes making a turn in the 1999 Daytona 200 race.

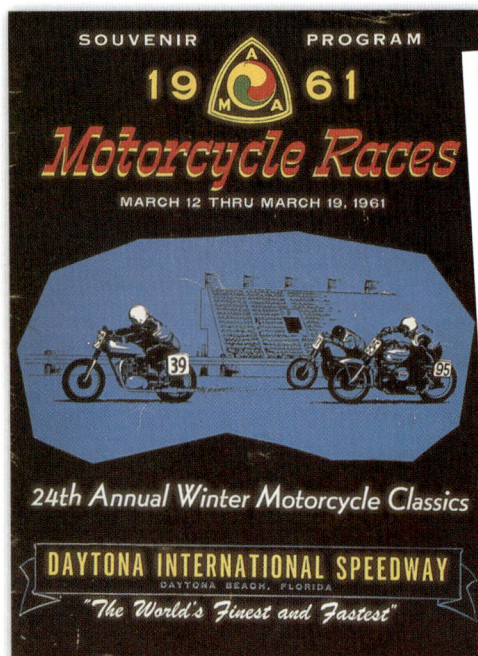

SOUVENIR PROGRAM

19 61

Motorcycle Races

MARCH 12 THRU MARCH 19, 1961

24th Annual Winter Motorcycle Classics

DAYTONA INTERNATIONAL SPEEDWAY
DAYTONA BEACH, FLORIDA
"The World's Finest and Fastest"

Program for the 1961 Motorcycle Races at the Daytona International Speedway.

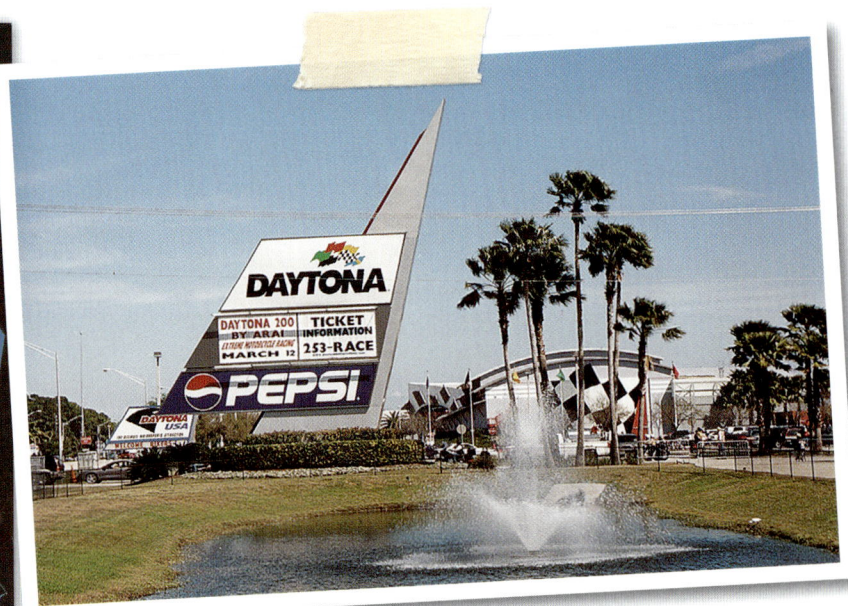

The Daytona International Speedway, home of the Daytona 200 Motorcycle Race and Daytona Supercross races.

Supercross is the prodigal son of motocross racing, an American phenomena born in 1971 that has grown to become the world's most popular form of off-road motorcycle racing. At that time, European riders dominated motocross racing, and the sport was just beginning to take hold in the United States.

The first design for the sport was a rugged, outdoor race track assembled on the infield of the Daytona International Speedway. The Supercross race was designed to be a supporting race of the highly successful Daytona 200 roadrace. East Coast motocross veteran Gary Bailey was commissioned to build a long, rough, bike-breaking circuit that was etched out of the grassy section of Daytona's trioval field. The Daytona Supercross track is similar to an outdoor national circuit. Supercross racing has grown explosively into a popular, serious, professional sport.

Supercross has changed dramatically since its conception in 1971, as have riders who shaped the sport. The riders from the early days would be amazed by the aerial acrobatics and seventy-one-foot leaps performed routinely by modern supercross pilots.

The drivers and motorcycle type for the Daytona Supercross (250-CC class) races at the Daytona International Speedway are shown in Table 3 (next page).

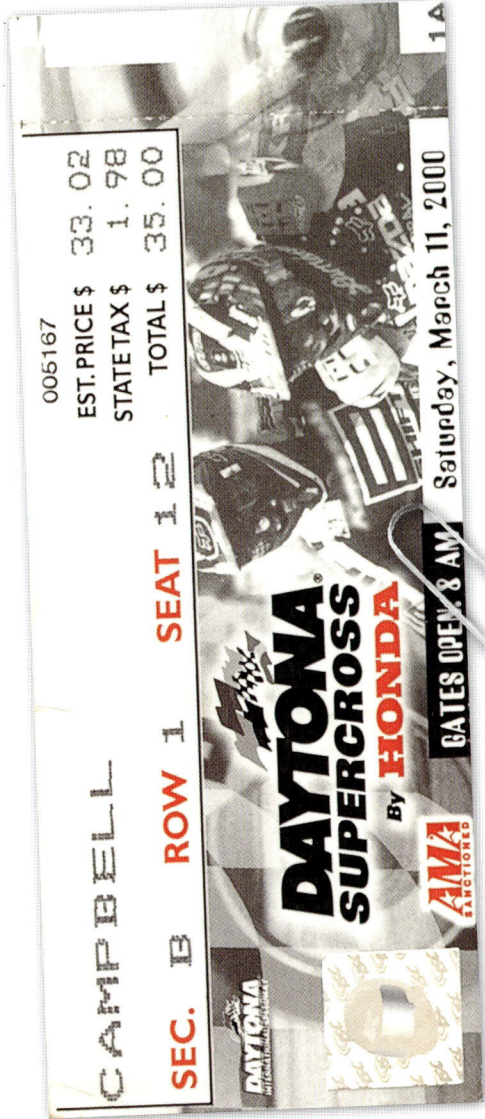

TABLE 3

YEAR	DRIVER	MOTORCYCLE TYPE
1971	Grannar Lindstrom	Husqvarna
1972	Jimmy Weinert	Yamaha
1973	Bob Grossi	Husqvarna
1974	Pierre Karsmakers	Yamaha
1975	Jimmy Ellis	Can-Am
1976	Tony DiStefano	Suzuki
1977	Bob Hannah	Yamaha
1978	Marty Tripes	Honda
1979	Jimmy Weinert	Kawasaki
1980	Rex Staten	Yamaha
1981	Darrell Schaltz	Suzuki
1982	Darrell Schaltz	Honda
1983	Bob Hannah	Honda
1984	David Bailey	Honda
1985	Bob Hannah	Honda
1986	Rick Johnson	Honda
1987	Rick Ryan	Honda
1988	Rick Johnson	Honda
1989	Jeff Stanton	Honda
1990	Jeff Stanton	Honda
1991	Jeff Stanton	Honda
1992	Jeff Stanton	Honda
1993	Mike Kiedrowski	Kawasaki
1994	Mike Kiedrowski	Kawasaki
1995	Mike Kiedrowski	Kawasaki
1996	Jeremy McGrath	Honda
1997	Jeff Emig	Kawasaki
1998	Jeremy McGrath	Yamaha
1999	Jeremy McGrath	Yamaha
2000	Ricky Carmichael	Kawasaki
2001	Ricky Carmichael	Kawasaki
2002	Ricky Carmichael	Honda
2003	Ricky Carmichael	Honda
2004	Chad Reed	Yamaha
2005	Chad Reed	Yamaha
2006	Ricky Carmichael	Suzuki
2007	James Stewart	Kawasaki
2008	Kevin Windham	Honda

The Supercross racetrack at the Daytona International Speedway. It is a highly competitive arena for fast and tough dirt bikes. A monster.com blimp has a good view of the action on the racecourse.

SEC. B   ROW 1   SEAT 12   TOTAL $ 35.00

DAYTONA
SUPERCROSS

Supercross racing requires speed, agility and endurance from both machine and rider. The bikes used in Supercross racing are very light weight, but are built strong and rugged to take the abuse of jumps and landings. Action is what Supercross riders seek.

Young daredevil bikers leaping their way to the finish line at the Daytona Supercross. This exciting event is one of the most popular during Bike Week at Daytona Beach.

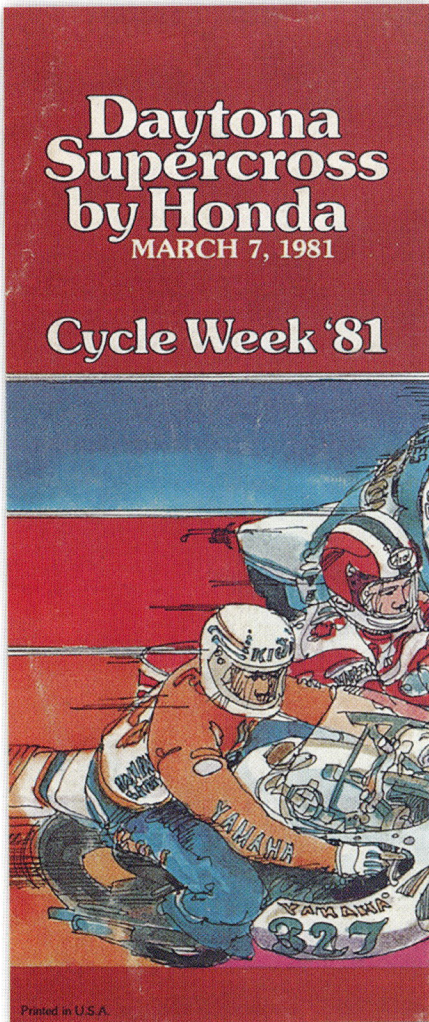
1981 Daytona Supercross brochure.

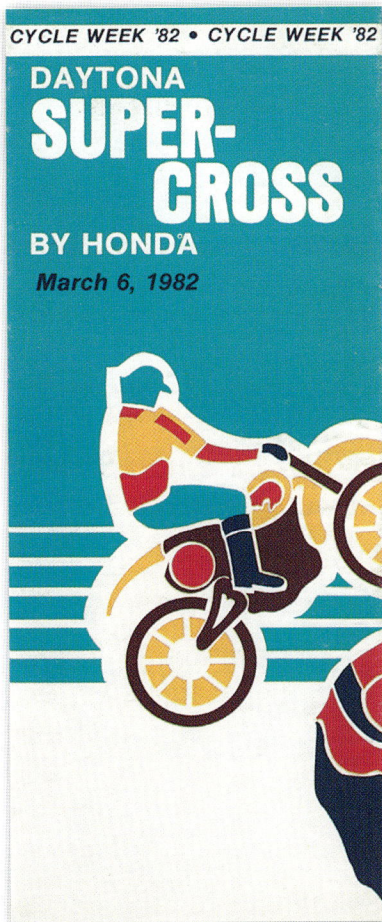
1982 Daytona Supercross brochure.

Program for the 2000 Daytona Supercross and the Daytona 200 races.

Close-ups of Daytona Supercross riders.

CHAPTER 12

TATTOOS, HELMETS, T-SHIRTS, & BIKE GRAPHICS

Tattoos

Regarded by the bikers who wear them as the ultimate form of personal expression, tattoo designs have evolved from pagan ornaments into a popular form of body art. Bikers wear such designs as skulls, beautiful ladies, butterflies, animals, flowers, weapons, exotic designs and a host of other striking figures.

Colorful body art arrangement.

Harley bikers are well known for their personalized helmets, lively T-shirts, black leather jackets, and tattoos. These elements are part of the entertainment during events where bikers congregate.

Tattooing has been called "the second-oldest profession."

Someday I'm going to get a new outfit.

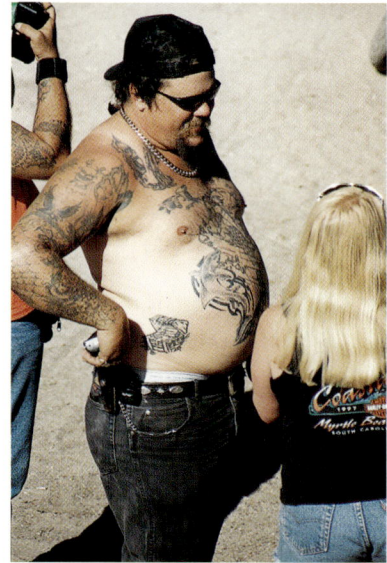

Full body art.

Look at *my* tattoo!

I dress to show off my tattoos.

A graying biker with tattoos.

I'll bet I have more tattoos than you have.

Unusual graphic art.

I've had a bad day!

The purpose of a motorcycle helmet is to disperse the energy of a crash impact before it reaches the riders head. The helmet's liner does this by crushing at a controlled rate. But for most bikers, it's fashion over function, and the helmet soon becomes a place for personal expression and a good laugh. Stickers, logos, and sayings adorn most bikers' headgear. This biker is wearing a "shorty," or half helmet.

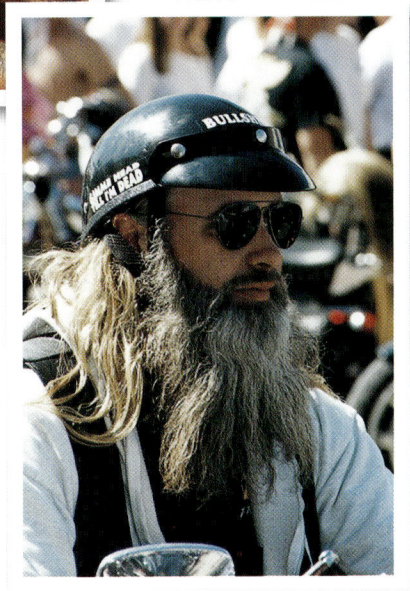
Biker wearing a cropped helmet.

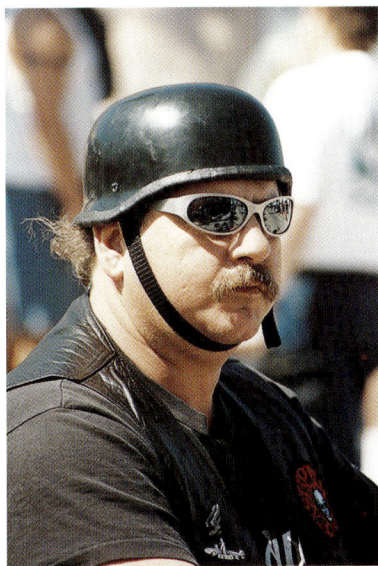
This helmet is called a "brain bucket."

A customized helmet.

I bought this helmet last year while attending Bike Week. I personalized it with my favorite stickers.

Some helmet stickers.

BAD TO THE BONE

BORN TO BE A BIKER

More helmet stickers: Hairdo by Helmet, I like My Women a Little on the Trashy Side, I'm not cheap, There's No Life Like Low Life, Bad Is Fun, Iron Horse Saloon, White Trash, Life's Too Short to Ride with Ugly Women!, Life's Too Short to Ride with Ugly Men!, Have You Had Your Spanking Today, Tattoos are more than Skin Deep!, I'm not totally useless—I can be used as a Bad Example!, Will Work For Sex, Bikers have more fun than people do!, and Boot Hill Saloon.

T-Shirt merchandising serves as another reminder of the increasing popularity of Daytona Beach's Bike Week. Twenty years ago, most of the popular biker bars sold their T-Shirts from shelf behind the counter. Today, these businesses have many tables, rooms or outside tents selling merchandise. In addition, there are hundreds of independent vendors that offer a wide variety of biker merchandise.

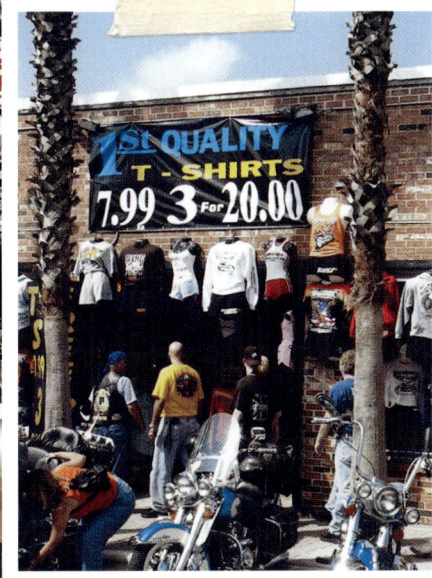

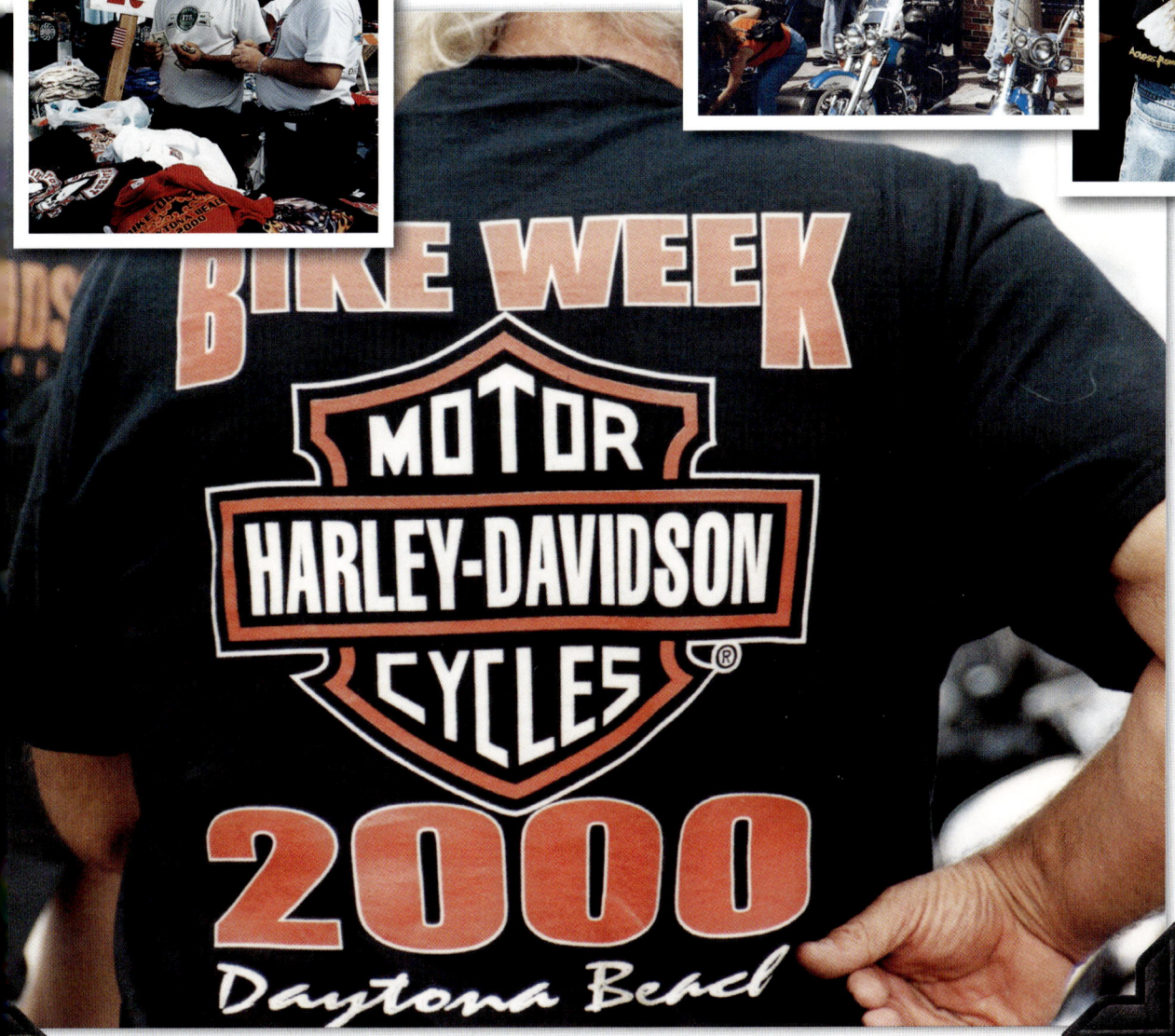

T-Shirts and other merchandise are sold by most of the biker bars in the Daytona Beach area. Shown is a Boot Hill Saloon T-Shirt.

Harley-Davidson T-Shirts are popular during Bike Week, sporting slogans like *God rides a Harley* and *Harley-Davison: If I had to explain, you wouldn't understand*. Harley riders like to advertise their loyalty.

A Biketoberfest T-Shirt.

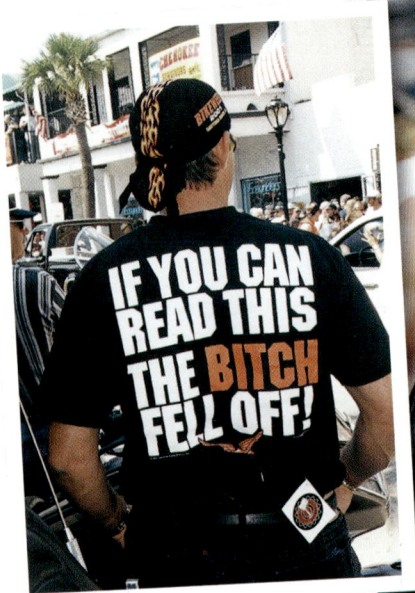

Does Not Play Well With Others.
An eye-catching design.

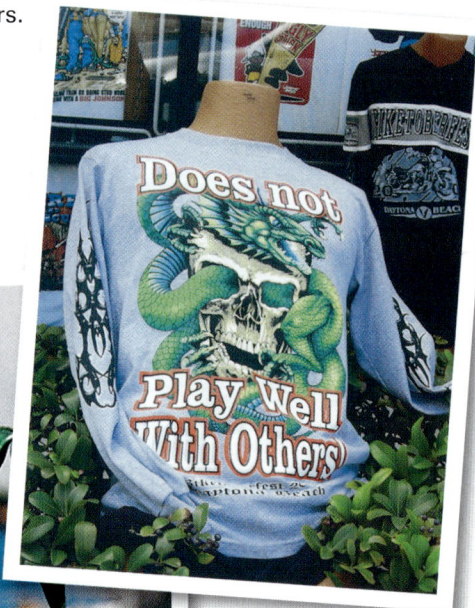

This guy probably rides alone.

A Bike Week Bar Tour T-Shirt.

Just to prove you were there!

Cool T-SHIRTS

A Cabbage Patch T-Shirt featuring two coleslaw-wrestling girls.

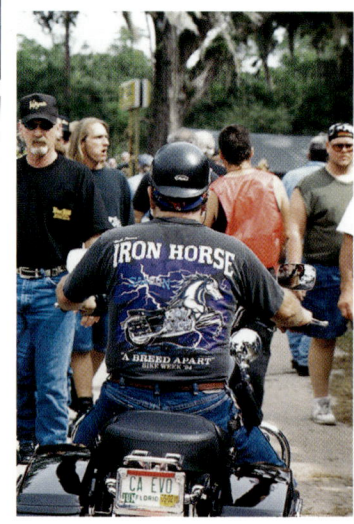

An official "Iron Horse Saloon" T-Shirt.

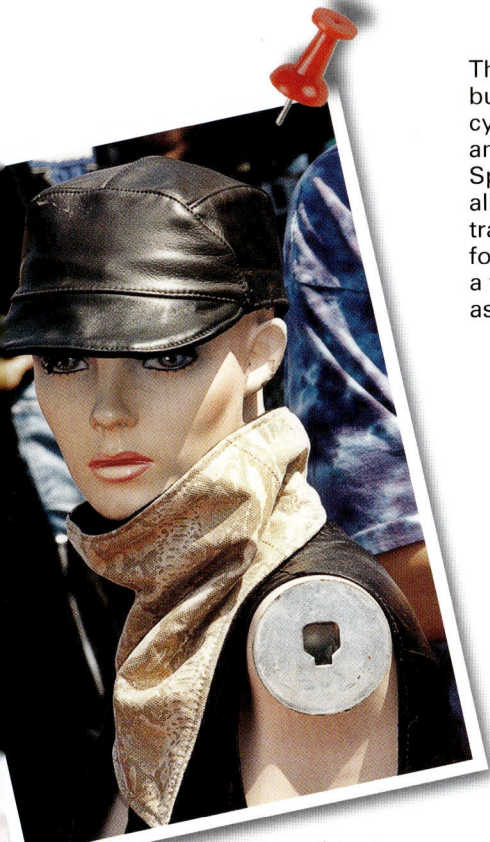

The right riding gear not only looks good, but also functions well. The job of motorcycle apparel is to shut out the elements and keep the rider comfortable and dry. Sporting and racing leathers are usually stylish and heavily protective. The traditional cruiser jacket takes on many forms. Shown here is a leather cap, and a faux snake-skin collar that can double as a protective facemask.

Horny's HardWear.

A classy biker outfit.

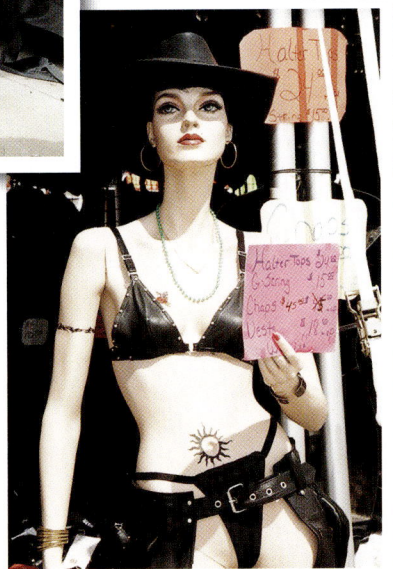

Bike Week in Daytona Beach is a good place to buy items for both riders and bikes. Here, a lady biker shops the dozens of vendors that line Main Street.

A biker's leather beach outfit!

Finally! A place where I can wear lots of leather without being accused of soliciting!

Colorful dragon bike graphics.

The trend to customize motorcycles developed in California during the 1960s.

Ladies, snakes and tigers are popular on Harley-Davidson motorcycle gas tanks.

A pistol-packing gal bike graphic decorates this Harley gas tank.

Could this biker be from the South?

A grinch-like character decorates this gas tank.

A colorful gas tank design.

A gambler's bike graphic.

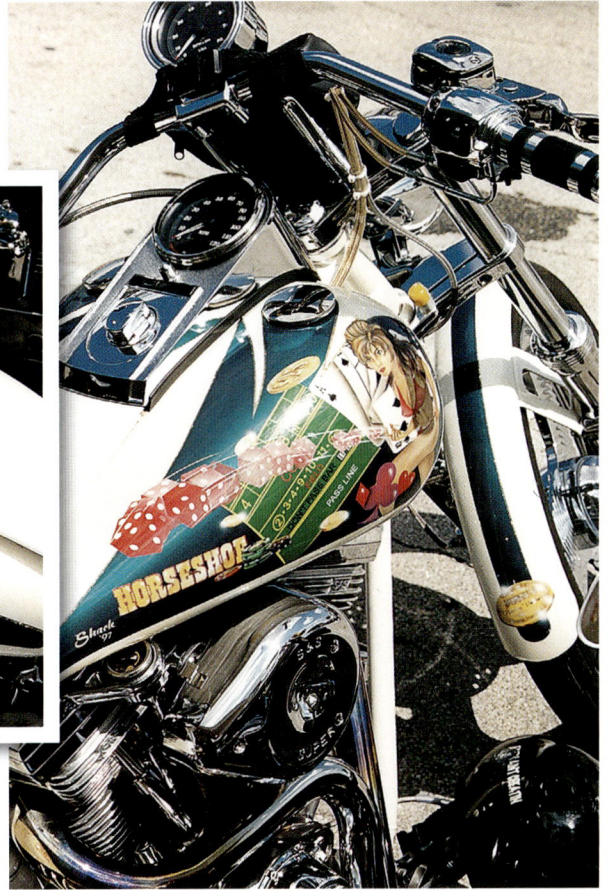

A bike that would be very popular in Las Vegas.

I never drink and ride. I wouldn't want to mess up my bike graphics.

Another colorful bike graphic.

3-D graphics decorate this Florida bike.

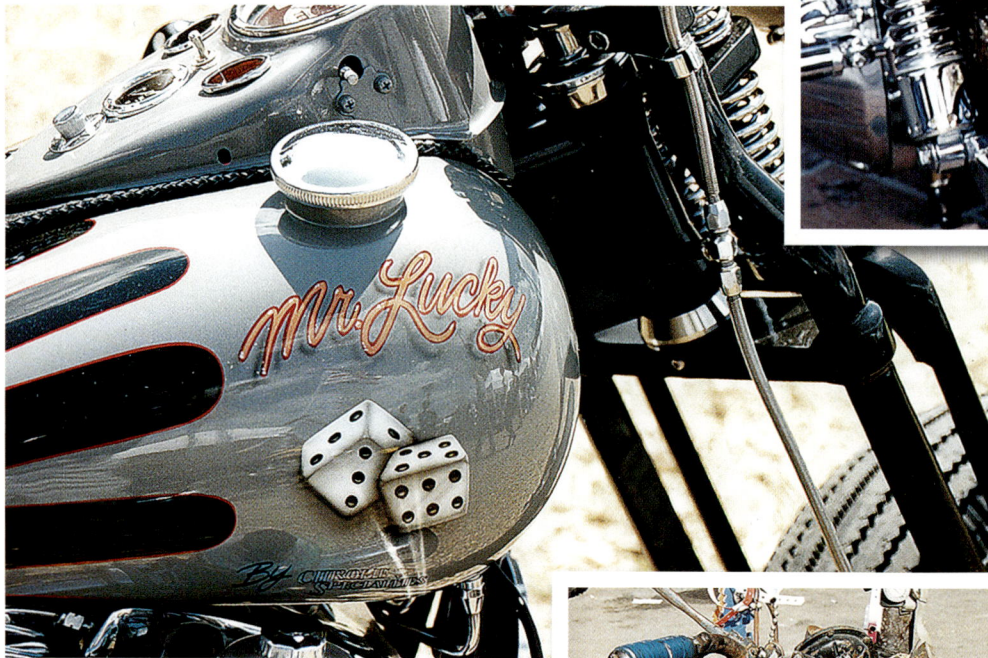

Hope this biker is a Craps player.

For those who don't like fancy paint and shiny chrome, building a ratbike provides the perfect opportunity to let the imagination run wild. This one belongs to Free Willi, a singing Bike Week regular.

Remember when water was $1.00 a bottle?

Daytona Beach's Biketoberfest weekend has grown into a major event.

The traffic during October's Biketoberfest runs at a fast trickle compared to the clutch-slipping crawl of March's Bike Week. About 100,000 bikers attend Biketoberfest, a fifth of the Bike Week crowd.

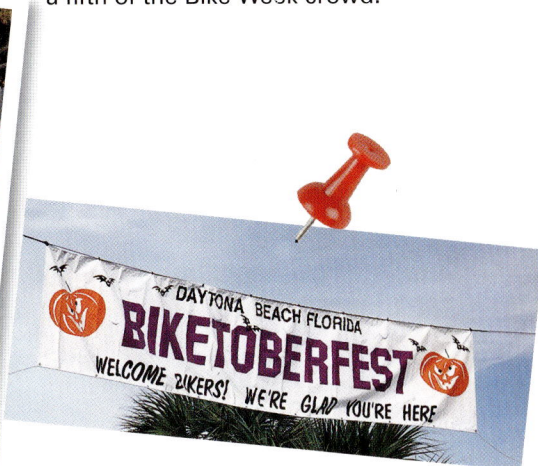

Daytona Beach welcomes bikers to Biketoberfest.

A Biketoberfest Main Street Scene.

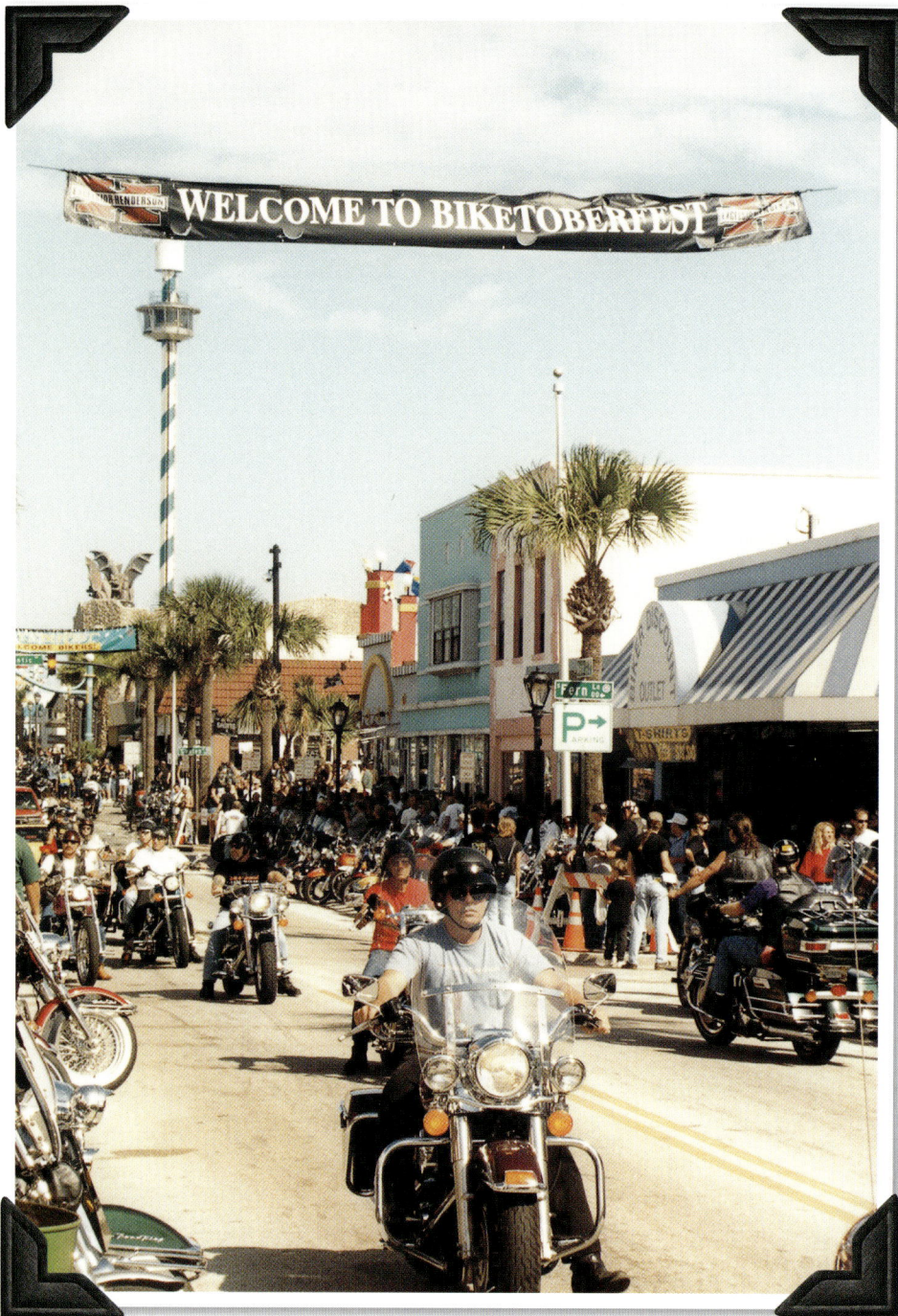

This view shows the Boardwalk Tower.

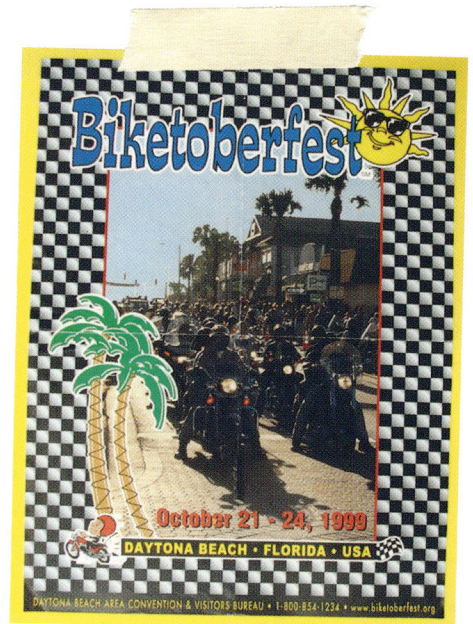

1999 Biketoberfest Poster.

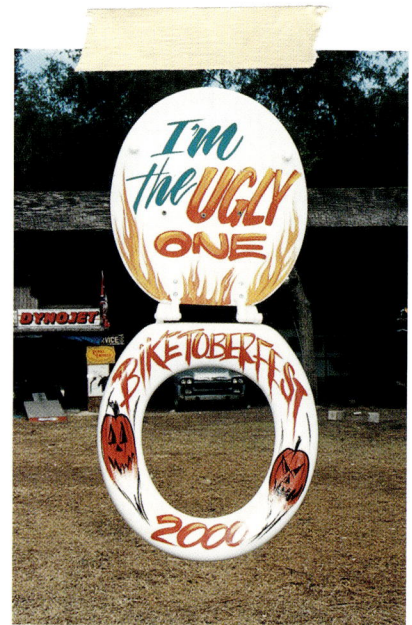

Just another pretty face.

Two-wheel thunder is held at the Daytona International Speedway during Biketoberfest. Top Championship Cup Series and American Sportbike Racing Association riders compete in season-ending finales as full-throttle racing takes on the twists and turns of the speedway 3.56-mile road course. Racing program.

Biketoberfest event booklets.

Indian motorcycle exhibit and demo ride area at the Daytona International Speedway.

Follow me! A demo-ride group. The author's daughter, Laura, is directing the motorcycle riders in this view.

Kawasaki motorcycle exhibit and demo ride area at the Daytona International Speedway.

Yamaha motorcycle exhibit and demo area at the Daytona International Speedway.

Demo rides are popular throughout Bike Week and Bike-toberfest. These rides give bikers a chance to drive new motorcycles from the major manufacturers.

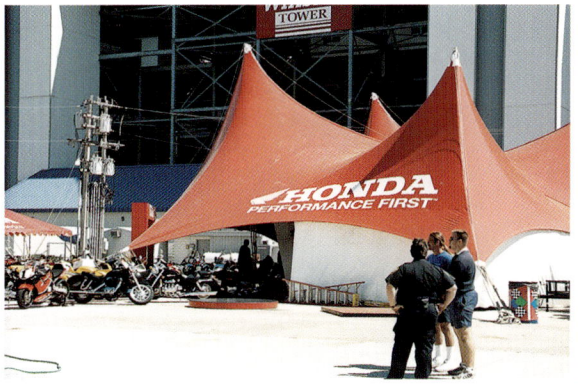

Honda motorcycle exhibit and demo ride area at the Daytona International Speedway.

Bike Week event booklets.

Bike Week (handwritten)

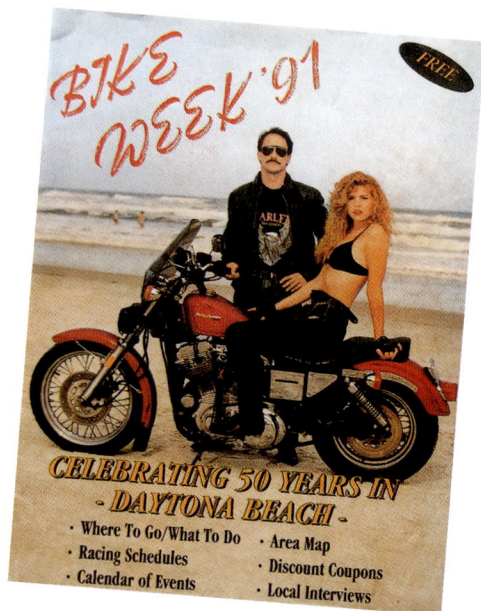

Bike Week 1991, celebrating 50 years in Daytona Beach.

Suzuki motorcycle exhibit and demo ride area at the Daytona International Speedway.

Two bikers enjoying the fabulous beach scenery at Daytona Beach.

A patriotic Harley biker.

Nice Bike!

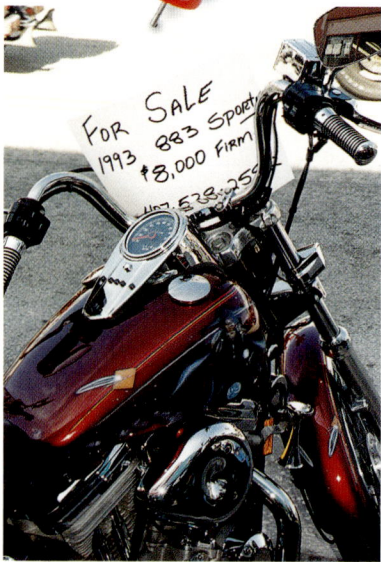

There are always lots of bikes for sale during biking events.

Bike Week in Daytona Beach is just like Mardi Gras in New Orleans.

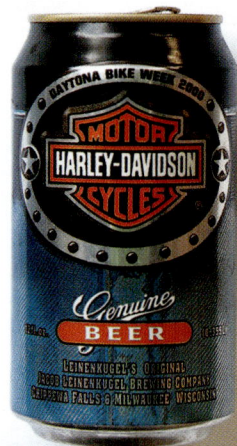

Buy a ticket and win a bike! The United Way and other charities find Bike Week patrons in the mood to take a chance, spend some money, and have a little fun with contests and raffles that happen to help local causes at the same time.

A bike-riding-in-a-cage exhibit. This action was located in the infield at the Daytona International Speedway during a Daytona 200 race.

Daytona Bike Week 2000 Beer Can. This Harley-Davidson branded beer was not brewed in the plant that manufactured V-twin motors; however it was brewed in Milwaukee, home of Harley's corporate offices. It came in cans complete with the famous Harley-Davidson logo. Produced in limited quantities, it quickly became a collectible.

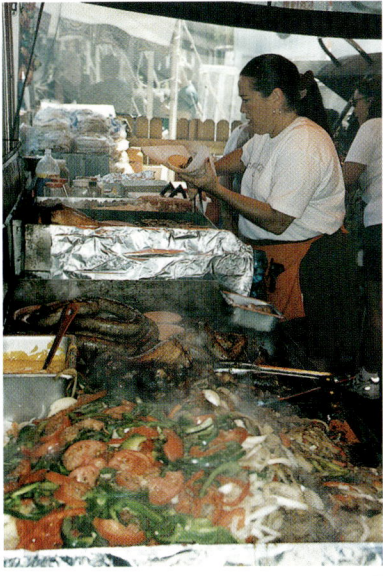

During Bike Week, food vendors are present wherever there are visiting bikers.

Custom bikes on display.

Cycle World Daytona is a large motorcycle dealer, located at 2900 Bellevue Avenue, representing Honda, Suzuki and Yamaha bikes, accessories, and parts.

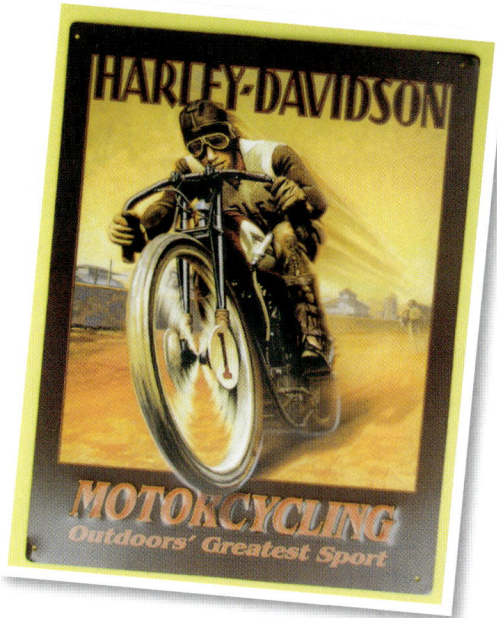

Harley-Davidson tin sign.

This biker-alligator statue has seen better days.

After Bike Week, Main Street is suddenly just another city byway, with plenty of available parking and an eerie quiet. The sidewalk vendors are gone, the bikers have all but cleared out, and there are only a handful of open businesses that sell T-shirts, biker jackets, or beer. It is sad to see the vendors pack up and go, but the popularity and scale of this massive biker party guarantees that in March, it will all be back.

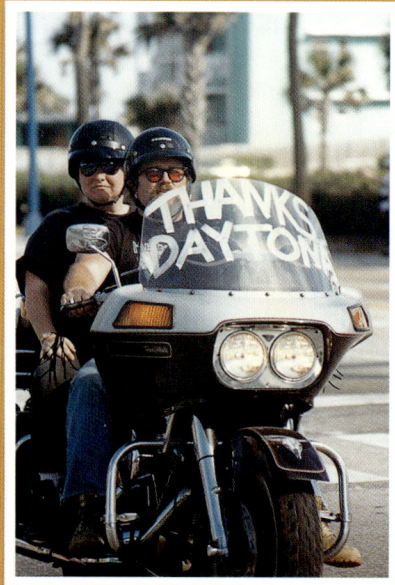

Thanks, Daytona!

Ash, Kevin. *BMW Motorcycles*. London, England: Carlton Books, 2001.

Bacon, Roy. *The Illustrated Motorcycle Legends*. Edison, New Jersey: Chartwells Books, Inc., 1995.

Bianchi, Luigi and Marco Masetti. *Ducati: 50 Golden Years*. Somerset, England: Haynes Publishing, 1999.

Bolfert, Thomas C. *The Big Book of Harley-Davidson*. Milwaukee, Wisconsin: Harley Davidson, Inc., 1991.

Bishop, George. *The Encyclopedia of Motorcycling*. New York, New York: G. P. Putnam's Sons, 1980.

Bonnello, Joe. *Supercross*. Osceola, Wisconsin: Motorbooks International Publishers, 1997.

Brown, Roland. *A-Z of Motorcycles*. New York, New York: Lorenz Books, 1999.

Brown, Roland. *The Encyclopedia of Motorcycles*. New York, New York: Smithmark Publishers, 1996.

Carrick, Peter, *Motorcycle Racing*. New York, New York: Hamlyn Publishing Group Ltd., 1969.

Clymer, Floyd. *A Treasury of Motorcycles of the World*. New York: New York: McGraw-Hill Book Company, 1965.

Clymer, Floyd. *Historical Motor Scrapbooks: Volumes 1 through 7*. Los Angeles, California: Clymer Motors, 1944-1954.

Davidson, Jean. *Growing Up Harley-Davidson: Memoirs of a Motorcycle Dynasty*. Stillwater, Minnesota: Voyageur Press, 2001.

Davidson, Jean. *Harley-Davidson Family Album*. Stillwater, Minnesota: Voyageur Press, 2003.

Daytona 200 program. Daytona Beach, Florida: International Speedway Corporation, 1997.

Dregni, Michael, Editor. *This Old Harley*. Stillwater, Minnesota: Voyageur Press, 2000.

Dregni, Michael. *The Spirit of the Motorcycle*. Stillwater, Minnesota: Voyageur Press, Inc., 2000.

Dunbar, Leila. *Motorcycle Collectibles*. Atglen, Pennsylvania: Schiffer Publishing Ltd., 1996.

Emde, Don. *The Daytona 200: The History of America's Premier Motorcycle Race.* Aliso Viego, California: Don Emde Productions, 2004.

Gottesman, Eric. *Classic Tattoo Designer*. Mineola, New York: Dover Publications, Inc., 2003.

Green, William. *Harley-Davidson: The Living Legend*. New York, New York: Crescent Books, 1994.

Harley-Davidson Lore: Origins Through Panhead: 1903-1965. San Francisco, California: Chronicle Books, 1999.

Hatfield, Jerry. *Indian Motorcycle Photographic History*. Osceola, Wisconsin: Motorbooks International, 1993.

Henshaw, Peter and Ian Kerr. *The Encylopedia Of The Harley-Davidson*. Edison, New Jersey: Chartwell Books, 2007.

Henshaw, Peter. *A Century of Harley-Davidson*. Wayne, New Jersey: Stoeger Publishing Company, 1998.

Jones, Jr., Bob and Tim Richmond. *Run To The Sun: Bike Week-Daytona*. Richmond, Virginia: Tim Richmond & Bob Jones, Jr., 1988.

Kanter, Buzz. *Indian Motorcycles*. Osceola, Wisconsin: MBI Publishing Company, 1993.

Knittel, Stefan and Roland Slabon. *BMW Motorcycle*. Osceola, Wisconsin: MBI Publishing, 1996.

La Fontaine, Bruce. *Motorcycles*. New York, New York: Dover Publishing, Inc., 1995.

Marselli, Mark. *Classic Harley-Davidson Big Twins*. Osceola, Wisconsin: Motorbooks International, 1994.

Mauk, Jonathan V. *The Gallery of Legends Book*. Daytona Beach, Florida: International Speedway Corporation, 1995.

McDiarmid, Mac. *Harley-Davidson: A Visual History*. London, England: Anness Publishing Ltd., 2001.

Motorcyclist Magazine Editors. *Motorcycles*. New York, New York: Penguin group, 2004.

Neely, William. *Daytona U.S.A.* Tucson, Arizona: Aztex Corporation, 1979.

On Two Wheels: The Illustrated Encyclopedia of Motorcycles. 20 Volumes. Freeport, New York: Marshall Cavendish Ltd., 1979.

Page, Roby. *Bike Week at Daytona Beach: Bad Boys and Fancy Toys*. Jackson, Mississippi: University Press of Mississippi, 2005.

Racer X Illustrated editors. *The Way of the Motorcrosser*, New York, New York: Harry N. Abrams, Inc., 2003.

Rae, Rusty. *The World's Biggest Motorcycle Race: The Daytona 200*. Minneapolis, Minnesota: Lerner Pub. Co., 1978.

Spencer, Donald D. *Black Leather: A Pictorial History of Bike Week in Daytona Beach*. Ormond Beach, Florida: Camelot Publishing, 2002.

Stewart, Gail. *Motorcycle Racing: Super-Charged!* Mankato, Minnesota: Crestwood House, 1998.

Ten Days In March: Celebrating Bike Week '91. Video. WCEU-TV/15 Public TV Station, 1991.

Tuthill, William R. *Speed On Sand*. Ormond Beach, Florida: Ormond Beach Historical Trust, Inc., 1978.

Tuthill, William R., Don Bostrom, Carolyn Jernigan, Gordon Kipp and Ellen Rabin. *Speed On Sand, Revised Edition*. Ormond Beach, Florida: Ormond Beach Historical Trust, 2002.

Vanderheuvel, Cornelis. *Pictorial History of Japanese Motorcycles*. Bideford Devon: Bay View Books Ltd., 1997.

Walker, Mick. *History of Motorcycles*. New York, New York: Stirling Publishing Co., 1997.

Wilson, Hugo. *The Ultimate Motorcycle Book.* New York, New York: DK Publishing, 1993.

Youngblood, Ed. *A Century of Indian*. St. Paul, Minnesota: MBI Publishing Company, 2001.

Youngblood, Ed, Editor. *Heroes Of Harley-Davidson*. St. Paul, Minnesota: Motorbooks International, 2003.

INDEX